THE GLOBAL HISTORY SERIES

Leften Stavrianos, *Northwestern University*
General Editor

This series aims to present history in global perspective, going beyond national or regional limitations, and dealing with overriding trends and forces. The various collections of original materials span the globe, range from prehistoric times to the present, and include anthropology, economics, political science, and religion, as well as history.

Charles W. Forman, editor of this volume, is D. Willis James Professor of Missions at Yale University. The son and grandson of missionaries to India, Professor Forman has traveled widely and has been prominently identified with the work of Christian missions. He is the author of *A Faith for the Nations, The Nation and the Kingdom,* and articles for numerous publications.

Also in the Global History Series

**CHRISTIANITY
IN THE NON-WESTERN WORLD**

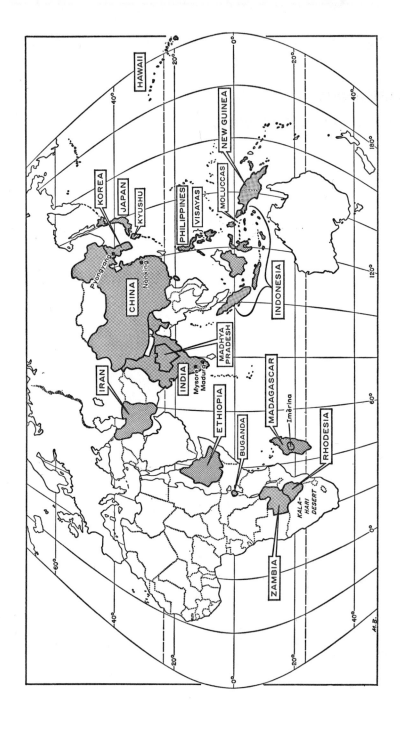

CHRISTIANITY
IN THE NON-WESTERN WORLD

EDITED BY CHARLES W. FORMAN

 Prentice-Hall, Inc. / *Englewood Cliffs, N.J.*

© 1967 by Prentice-Hall, Inc.,
Englewood Cliffs, New Jersey.

A SPECTRUM BOOK.

Library of Congress Catalog Card Number 67-14851
Printed in the United States of America

C

Current printing (last number):
10 9 8 7 6 5 4 3 2 1

PREFACE

Christianity has been commonly regarded as a religion of the West. Such an identification, however, fails to do justice to the cosmopolitan nature of Christianity and to the diversified nature of the non-Western world. Christianity, which found its roots and beginnings in Asia, and which during ancient times had some of its areas of greatest strength in Asia and Africa, has never ceased to lead part of its life on those continents. Scattered throughout Asian and African history are the traces of Christian activity, sometimes faint and forgotten, at other times clear and impressive.

The diversity of the non-Western world is marked not only by the fact that it includes Christianity within its religious heritage but also by the diverse stamps it has put on the Christian faith. For the Western observer the Christianity of Asia and Africa is at times exceedingly strange. (The first two selections in the readings that follow describe two of the most unusual—from the Western perspective—of these forms.) At other times, especially in periods of Western ascendency, the features familiar in Western Christianity have been faithfully and even slavishly repeated. Yet even these periods have had their adaptations and deviations.

Most of the story of Christianity in the non-Western world has been a part of the story of the contacts between East and West (the East as used here designating Asia and Africa, not Eastern Europe). There are, however, some forms of Eastern Christianity that play no role in the East-West relationship, that have all their lives been embedded in the East with no Western contacts. For the most part, however, non-Western Christianity has had to live constantly in terms of the East-West tension, has always had to face the question of whether or not there should be distinctively non-Western Christianity.

The materials available for readings from the history of non-Western Christianity are far too extensive for the whole to be properly represented in this book. A more specific purpose must guide this selection and so the present volume is concerned with exposing the nature of non-Western Christianity and with showing how it has fitted into the East-West dialogue that has been an increasingly dominant theme of world history. We examine first, through an outstanding example, something of the nature of the Christianity that has always been embedded in the East (Part I, 1). We then turn to the early modern experiments in creating a new non-western Christianity (Part II, 2-3) and also look at some early modern examples of uncreative importations from the West (Part II, 4-5). The main emphasis of the readings falls on the nineteenth and twentieth centuries. The nineteenth century and the years immediately following marked the great period of Western missionary ascendency. We look at examples of the life and work of the missionaries and their various forms of social service (Part III, 7, 10, 16-18). We see how in some cases the East accepted nearly all the missionaries brought (Part III, 8-9) and how in other cases it worked out modifications of their church structures, their theological positions, and their evangelistic and ceremonial forms (Part III, 11-15). Finally, examples of the emergence of a newly independent non-Western Christianity in the mid-twentieth century are given to illustrate the Eastern church's encounter with competitive forces in its environment (Part IV, 19-24) and also to illustrate something of the self-expressive life that it is presently developing (Part IV, 25-28).

The readings are taken in nearly all cases from the writings of men and women who were participants in or eye-witnesses to the events they describe. By employing such direct contact with the actors in the drama it is hoped that this history will come to life for the reader with something of its original intensity and unsettledness.

C.W.F.

CONTENTS

CHRISTIANITY
IN THE NON-WESTERN WORLD

INTRODUCTION

The most enduring segments of non-Western Christianity are the ancient churches of western Asia and northeast Africa. For long centuries the Greek Church, the Armenian Church, the Syrian Church, and the Coptic Church dominated the lands around the eastern end of the Mediterranean and as far south as Ethiopia. Further east in Mesopotamia the Nestorian Church developed, and though it did not dominate the area it represented an important and influential minority faith which spread through the business and professional classes as far east as Central Asia and China.

These churches were the bearers of much of the ancient culture of the East. They continued to represent that venerable Eastern tradition after the triumph of Islam brought a new configuration to Eastern life. To describe such churches as non-Western suggests, of course, a ridiculously provincial point of view. They are churches of the East with a life of their own, quite independent of and often antedating that of the West and its churches. The pressures of Islam have, however, gradually reduced them in size till only a shrunken remnant is left. The Nestorians are reduced to some thirty-five thousand in Iraq and nearby Syria. The old Syrian Church has between fifty and a hundred thousand adherents in its homeland and another 350,000 in South India. The Armenians have been scattered abroad so that only some 300,000 remain in Western Asia. The Copts still number about a million and form a significant minority of the Egyptian population. The ancient patriarchates which continue the Greek connection and tradition—Constantinople, Antioch, Jerusalem, and Alexandria—command the allegiance of about 100,000 each, except for Antioch, which has three times that number. In addition, there are branches of all of these churches which have come into communion with the Roman Catholic Church. In the Middle East these are numerous only in Syria and Lebanon, where they number half a million members in each land. Little Lebanon, because of its Roman Catholics (chiefly Maronites) and its adherents of the Patriarch of Antioch, is about half Christian in population and operates nationally in terms of a co-operative arrangement between Christians and Muslims. In the other countries Christians exist only as a small, deeply entrenched minority group.

In one land alone does the old church dominance still survive; that land is Ethiopia. Ethiopian Christianity dates from the first half of the fourth century. Until recently it was technically a dependency of the Coptic Church in Egypt, but it has long been much larger and more influential than its mother church. In fact, with four million adherents, it is the largest of the ancient churches of the East. Isolated for centuries by the Islamic power to the north, it has developed a unique life which shows many traits more closely related to its African environment and its Semitic neighbors than to the rest of Christendom. The difficulty in establishing Christian marriage and the shape of the church buildings reveal the African environment, while the maintenance of much of the Jewish Levitical law and the practice of circumcision are signs of the Semitic neighborhood.

Because of its outstanding size and its unique characteristics this Church deserves to be better known in the Western world. The following account of the Church, given by an eighteenth-century explorer, describes a time when the country was still almost entirely isolated from the rest of the world. In more recent years outside influences have grown enormously, but the Church remains highly conservative, and most of the features described by this author are characteristic of it even today.

1 / THE ETHIOPIAN CHURCH

There is no country in the world where there are so many churches as in Abyssinia [Ethiopia]. Though the country is very mountainous, and consequently the view much obstructed, it is very seldom you see less than five or six churches, and, if you are on a commanding ground, five times that number. Every great man that dies thinks he has atoned for all his

From James Bruce, *Travels to Discover the Source of the Nile, in the Years 1768, 1769, 1770, 1771, 1772, and 1773* (Dublin: Wiliam Porter, 1791), III, pp. 642-48, 650-51, 664, 669-71, 680.

wickedness if he leaves a fund to build a church, or has built one in his lifetime. The king builds many. Wherever a victory is gained, there a church is erected in the very field stinking with the putrid bodies of the slain. Formerly this was only the case when the enemy was Pagan or Infidel; now the same is observed when the victories are over Christians.

The situation of a church is always chosen near running water, for the convenience of their purifications and ablutions, in which they observe strictly the Levitical law. They are always placed upon the top of some beautiful, round hill, which is surrounded entirely with rows of the oxycedrus, or Virginia cedar, which grows here in great beauty and perfection, and is called Arz. There is nothing adds so much to the beauty of the country as these churches and the plantations about them.

In the middle of this plantation of cedars is interspersed, at proper distances, a number of those beautiful trees called Cusso, which grow very high, and are all extremely picturesque.

All the churches are round, with thatched roofs; their summits are perfect cones; the outside is surrounded by a number of wooden pillars, which are nothing else than the trunks of the cedar-tree, and are placed to support the edifice, about eight feet of the roof projecting beyond the wall of the church, which forms an agreeable walk, or colonnade, around it in hot weather, or in rain. The inside of the church is in several divisions according as is prescribed by the law of Moses. The first is a circle somewhat wider than the inner one; here the congregation sit and pray. Within this is a square, and that square is divided by a veil or curtain, in which is another very small division answering to the holy of holies. This is so narrow that none but the priests can go into it. You are barefooted whenever you enter the church, and, if bare-footed, you may go through every part of it, if you have any such curiosity, provided you are pure, i.e. have not been concerned with women for twenty-four hours before, or touched carrion or dead bodies (a curious assemblage of ideas), for in that case you are not to go within the precincts, or outer circumference of the church, but stand and say your prayers at an awful distance among the cedars.

All persons of both sexes, under Jewish disqualifications, are obliged to observe this distance; and this is always a place belonging to the church, where, unless in Lent, you see the greatest part of the congregation; but this is left to your own conscience, and, if there was either great inconvenience in the one situation, or great satisfaction in the other, the case would be otherwise.

When you go to the church you put off your shoes before your first entering the outer precinct; but you must leave a servant there with them, or else they will be stolen, if good for anything, by the priests and monks before you come out of the church. At entry you kiss the threshold, and two door-posts, go in and say what prayer you please; that finished, you come out again, and your duty is over. The churches are full of pictures, painted on parchment, and nailed upon the walls, in a manner little less slovenly than you see paltry prints in beggarly country ale-houses. There has been always a sort of painting known among the scribes, a daubing much inferior to the worst of our sign-painters. Sometimes, for a particular church, they get a number of pictures of saints, or skins of parchment, ready finished from Cairo, in a stile very little superior to these performances of their own. They are placed like a frize, and hung in the upper part of the wall. St. George is generally there with his dragon, and St. Demetrius fighting a lion. There is no choice in their saints, they are both of the Old and New Testament, and those that might be dispensed with from both. There is St. Pontius Pilate and his wife; there is St. Balaam and his ass; Samson and his jaw-bone; and so of the rest. But the thing that surprised me most was a kind of square-miniature upon the front of the head-piece, or mitre, of the priest, administering the sacrament at Adowa, representing Pharaoh on a white horse plunging in the Red Sea, with many guns and pistols swimming upon the surface of it around him.

Nothing embossed, nor in relief, ever appears in any of their churches; all this would be reckoned idolatry, so much so that they do not wear a cross, as has been represented, on the top of the ball of the sendick, or standard, because it casts a shade; but there is no doubt that pictures have been used in their churches from the very earliest age of Christianity.

The Abuna [bishop] is looked upon as the patriarch of the Abyssinian church, for they have little knowledge of the coptic patriarch of Alexandria [by whom the Abuna, till recently always an Egyptian, was appointed]. We are perfectly ignorant of the history of these prelates for many years after their appointment. The first of these mentioned is Abuna Tecla Haimanout, who distinguished himself by the restoration of the royal family, and the regulations he made both in church and state . . . : a very remarkable, but wise regulation was then made, that the Abyssinians should not have it in their power to choose one of their own countrymen as Abuna.

Wise men saw the fallen state of literature among them; and unless opportunity was given, from time to time, for their priests to go abroad to Jerusalem for their instruction, and for the purpose of bringing the Abuna, Tecla Haimanout knew that very soon no set of people would be more shamefully ignorant than those priests, even in the most common dogmas of their profession. . . . As the Abuna very seldom understands the language, he has no share of the government, but goes to the palace on days of ceremony, or when he has any favour to ask or complaint to make. He is much fallen in esteem from what he was formerly, chiefly from his own little intrigues, his ignorance, avarice, and want of firmness. His greatest employment is in ordinations. A number of men and children present themselves at a distance, and there stand, from humility, not daring to approach him. He then asks who these are? and they tell him that they want to be deacons. On this, with a small iron cross in his hand, after making two or three signs, he blows with his mouth twice or thrice upon them, saying, "Let them be deacons." I saw once all the army of Begemder made deacons, just returned from shedding the blood of 10,000 men, thus drawn up in Aylo Meidan, and the Abuna standing at the church of St. Raphael, about a quarter of a mile distant from them. With these were mingled about 1000 women, who consequently having part of the same blast and brandishment of the cross, were as good deacons as the rest.

The same with regard to monks. A crowd of people, when he is riding, will assemble within 500 yards of him, and there begin a melancholy song. He asks who those men with beards are? they tell him they want to be ordained monks. After the same signs of the cross, and three blasts with his mouth, he orders them to be monks. But in ordaining priests, they must be able to read a chapter of St. Mark, which they do in a language he does not understand a word of. They then give the Abuna a brick of salt, to the value of perhaps six-pence, for their ordination; which, from the present given, the Jesuits maintained to be Simoniacal. . . . The monks here do not live in convents as in Europe, but in separate houses round their church, and each cultivates a part of the property they have in land. The priests have their maintenance assigned to them in kind, and do not labour. A steward, being a layman, is placed among them by the king, who receives all the rents belonging to the churches, and gives to the priests the portion that is their due; but neither the Abuna, nor any other churchman, has any business with the revenues of churches, nor can touch them.

. . . Since the conquest of Arabia and Egypt by Sultan Selim, in 1516, the communication between Abyssinia and these two countries hath been very precarious and dangerous, if not entirely cut off; and now as to doctrine, I am perfectly convinced they are in every respect to the full as great heretics as ever the Jesuits represented them. . . . The two natures in Christ, the two persons, their unity, their equality, the inferiority of the manhood, doctrines, and definitions of the time of St. Athanasius, are all wrapt up in tenfold darkness, and inextricable from amidst the thick clouds of heresy and ignorance of language. Nature is often mistaken for person, and person for nature; the same of the human substance. It is monstrous to hear their reasoning upon it. One would think, that every different monk, every time he talks, purposely broached some new heresy. Scarce one of them that ever I conversed with, and those of the very best of them, would suffer it to be said, that Christ's body was perfectly like ours. Nay, it was easily seen that, in their hearts, they went still further, and were very loth to believe, if they did believe it at all, that the body of the Virgin Mary and St. Anne were perfectly human. . . .

The Abyssinians receive the holy sacrament in both kinds in unleavened bread, and in the grape bruised with the husk together as it grows, so that it is a kind of marmalade, and is given in a flat spoon: whatever they may pretend, some mixture seems necessary to keep it from fermentation in the state that it is in. . . .

The Abyssinians are not all agreed about the state of souls before the resurrection of the body. The opinion which generally prevails is, that there is no third state; but that, after the example of the thief, the souls of good men enjoy the beatific vision immediately upon the separation from the body. But I must here observe, that their practice and books do both contradict this; for, as often as any person dies, alms are given, and prayers are offered for the souls of those departed, which would be vain did they believe they were already in the presence of God, and in possession of the greatest bliss possible, wanting nothing to complete it. . . .

I have already said, that the Agaazi, the predecessors of those people that settled in Tigré from the mountains of the Habab, were shepherds adjoining to the Red Sea; that they speak the language *Geez*, and are the only people in Abyssinia in possession of letters; that these are all circumcised, both men and women. The former term, as applied to men, is commonly known to every one the least acquainted with the Jewish history. The latter is, as far as I know, a rite merely Gentile, although in Africa, at least that part adjoining to Egypt and the Red Sea, it is much more known and more universally practised than the other. This I shall call *excision*. . . . Being pressed for the reason, they tell you it is because

Christ and the apostles were circumcised, tho' they do not hold it necessary to salvation. But it is the objection they constantly make against eating out of the same plate, or drinking out of the same cup with strangers, that they are uncircumcised, while, with the Egyptians or the Cophts, though equally strangers. they make no such difficulty. . . .

There is another ceremony with which I shall close, and this regards the women also, and I shall call it *incision*. This is an usage frequent, and still retained among the Jews, though positively prohibited by the law: "Thou shalt not cut thy face for the sake of, or on account of the dead." As soon as a near relation dies in Abyssinia, a brother or parent, cousin-german or lover, every woman in that relation, with the nail of her little finger, which she leaves long on purpose, cuts the skin of both her temples, about the size of a sixpence; and therefore you see either a wound or a scar in every fair face in Abyssinia; and in the dry season, when the camp is out, from the loss of friends they seldom have liberty to heal till peace and the army return with the rains.

II / THE SIXTEENTH AND SEVENTEENTH CENTURIES: EXPERIMENTATION AND RIGIDITY

INTRODUCTION

The ancient churches living under the pressures of Islam have engaged in little missionary activity through the centuries. Where they have been able to hold their own they have usually been content. Therefore, most of the further development of Christianity in Asia and Africa has necessarily been initiated by the Western churches. In late medieval times a number of missions were undertaken by Western monks and friars traveling to India and China. A considerable church was built up in China, but it disappeared in the period following the collapse of the Mongol rule. The missions also came to an end when the land routes across Asia, which had been opened up by the Mongols, were closed.

The discovery of the sea route to Asia by Vasco da Gama, however, inaugurated a fresh period of missionary activity. The sixteenth and seventeenth centuries constitute the most brilliant pages in the history of non-Western Christianity. The Portuguese and Spanish gave Christianity a prominent place in their imperial designs. Even when expansion was being pursued for strictly political and commercial ends, they were wont to embellish these with religious claims, and often they adopted religious goals out of deep conviction. The Spanish impact on the non-Western world was limited to the Philippines. But the Portuguese sponsored missionaries along the West African coast, where a Christian kingdom arose for a time on the Congo, and in the principal countries of Asia.

The newly founded order of Jesuits provided a wealth of workers for the Asian lands. One of the initial group of Jesuits picked by Loyola was Francis Xavier, the pioneer of his order in India, Malaya, the Moluccas,

Japan and even China, where he died while trying to find a way into the country. Franciscans, Dominicans, and others came, but the Jesuits dominated most of the Asian scene.

The brilliance of the period was due not only to rapid and heroic advances but also to a boldness of design and experimentation. This was a time when the greatest flexibility and adaptability were required of Western Christianity in its advance into Asia. The earlier isolation of Asian cultures had broken down with the discovery of maritime lines of communication, but the later mixture of cultures had not yet developed. The distinct civilizations of India, China, and Japan were in full flower. Portuguese, and later Dutch, domination of the sea lanes and a few trading ports did not shake the power of the imperial overlords who ruled India, China, and Japan. Hence, this was the one time when it was both possible to bring Western Christianity extensively to Asia and yet necessary to make Christianity thoroughly adaptable to Asian traditions. Earlier and later periods provided no such combination of circumstances conducive to experimentation.

Not all of Asia, to be sure, could be characterized in this way. In those few spots which Western powers ruled—Goa, the Philippines, the Moluccas, Malacca—such flexibility was not required, and in those areas there appeared the most wooden and conventional forms of Christianity, a Western facade with little creative communication between it and the traditional life around it.

The following readings provide glimpses of both the experimental creativity and the secure conventionality which expressed the double nature of non-Western Christianity in this period.

2 / THE MOST RADICAL EXPERIMENT

Two men stand out as the principal innovators of Asian Christianity: Matteo Ricci and Robert di Nobili. Both were Jesuits and both came from Italy. Their experiments resulted in controversies which wracked the Roman Catholic missions for generations. The disputes over the Chinese rites and the Malabar rites were carried in appeal after appeal to the papal court until they were finally settled by the suppression of the innovations long after both innovators were dead.

Ricci, after years of study and effort, established himself in high repute at the court of China. He and his successors played important roles in the astronomical and geographical work at court. Ricci accommodated

Christianity to Chinese life by allowing for the customary veneration of Confucius and of the ancestors among Chinese Christians. In this and other ways he tried to dewesternize the faith he taught. His efforts were not matched by any comparable experiments at the imperial court of India. The Jesuits who manned that mission engaged in long debates, after the traditional Muslim fashion, regarding the merits of the religions. Their black robes were a familiar part of the scene at the Mogul court during several reigns, but they contributed little in the way of new understandings or applications of their faith.

The radical experimentation in India took place not in the imperial centers of the North but in the holy city of the extreme South, the capital of a small kingdom, Madura. To that city there came, in 1606, the brilliant and dedicated young di Nobili.

Robert di Nobili and His Successors in South India

The opening acts in his campaign were dramatically conceived and skilfully executed. Through Madura there ran one day a striking piece of news. It was told how a strange ascetic from some far land had arrived, drawn to the holy city by its great repute, and that he had taken up his abode in the Brahman quarter of the city. Hindus are as prone to curiosity as other people, and soon visitors flocked to the house of the holy man to see what they should see, but only to find that the Brahman's servants would not permit their entrance. "The Master," they said, "is meditating upon God. He may not be disturbed." This merely whetted the people's desire, and the fame of the recluse quickly grew, whereupon the privacy was relaxed, and daily audiences were granted to a privileged few.

Seated cross-legged on a settee the Sannyasi [ascetic] was found by his visitors, conforming in everything to Brahman usage. Over his shoulder hung the sacred cord of Caste, only in his case it was a cord of five threads, three of gold to symbolise the Trinity, and two of silver representing the body and soul of our Lord, and from the cord was suspended a small cross. Conversation revealed the Sannyasi's learning, and observation and keen inquiry certified to his frugal and holy life. One meal a day, consisting of a little rice and milk and acrid vegetables, was all his food. Soon not only ordinary Brahmans came to see him, but nobles also: and a great bound in his reputation took place when on being invited to the palace by the King, the Sannyasi declined the in-

From J. N. Ogilvie, *The Apostles of India From the Days of St. Thomas to Modern Times* (London: Hodder and Stoughton Ltd., 1915), pp. 172-80, 187-88. Reprinted by permission of the publisher.

vitation, lest on going forth the purity of his soul should be sullied by his eyes lighting upon a woman! Never was a holier saint seen in Madura. Where the life bore such testimony to his holiness, how could his teaching be other than true! His statement that he was a "Roman Brahman" of the highest caste was accepted, and to remove any possible doubts that might linger, an ancient discoloured parchment was produced which showed how the "Brahmans of Rome" had sprung direct from the god Brahma, and were the noblest born of all his issue. To the genuineness of this document the Sannyasi solemnly swore, and with open minds the people listened to his teaching.

Book after book was written by the able and daring writer, in which he grafted a modified Christian doctrine on the Hindu stem. Most notable of all such efforts was the forging of a "Fifth Veda," to complete and crown the four Vedas received by Brahmans as direct revelations from heaven. It was an amazing piece of daring—as bold and hazardous as it would be for a Hindu to forge for Christian use a fifth gospel. Yet the forgery held its place for one hundred and fifty years!

Brahman disciples were soon freely won; baptisms became fairly numerous, though the identity of the rite with the baptism administered by earlier European missionaries was disguised; and so far as outward tokens went, the new missionary method was proving a success. Without a doubt progress was greatly facilitated by the highly significant concessions that were made to Hinduism, especially in connection with Caste. According to de Nobili, caste had little religious signification. To him it was in the main a social observance, and so regarding it he saw no reason for compelling his converts to break with their caste fellowship or observances. Writing in 1609 he states his position:

> By becoming a Christian, one does not renounce his caste, nobility, or usages. The idea that Christianity interferes with them has been impressed upon the people by the devil, and is the great obstacle to Christianity. It is this that has stricken the work of Father Fernandez with sterility.

From no like cause did sterility threaten de Nobili's own work. His converts retained the *Kudumi* or tuft of hair which marked the caste Hindu, they wore a sacred cord indistinguishable from that of their Hindu neighbours, and they bore an oval caste mark on their brow, the paste composing it being made of the ashes of sandal-wood instead of as formerly of the ashes of cow-dung. With such concessions to the usages and spirit of Hinduism, it is no marvel that the new method outstripped the old in visible results.

But even so the difficulties which the daring innovator had to face were many and serious. His very success provoked opposition, and the agility and resource which he displayed in the many conflicts that arose furnish convincing evidence of his rare ability. The opposition proceeded from three distinct quarters. As might have been expected, the Brahman priests were bitterly antagonistic to the foreign innovator, and though their hostility was, as a rule, discreetly veiled, ever and again the veil was lifted. They distrusted this "Roman Brahman," but could not prove their distrust to be well founded. In learning and in argument de Nobili easily outclassed and defeated them: and where other measures failed to convince, he contrived by judicious presents to conciliate either his opponents, or the civil rulers without whose backing the priests were powerless to hurt.

More serious was his difficulty with his own Christian converts, who seem to have had a slumbering uneasiness regarding their position. Between them and the Paravan [low caste] Christians, who were ministered to by Father Fernandez, there yawned a great gulf which it pleased them to consider impassable. In 1610, however, their equanimity was seriously disturbed by a Paravan Christian, who arrived from the Southern Coast, and in plain terms declared that there was no gulf separating the one body of Christians from the other. De Nobili's work was threatened with destruction. His converts were told by this bold Paravan that by their baptism they had forsaken their caste, and had become mere Parangis and Paravans: and still further that de Nobili himself was a Parangi [a term, derived from the name of the Franks, used to refer to Europeans generally but at that time to the Portuguese specifically]. Consternation reigned, and secessions at once began: and it was only by taking a solemn oath, in which he purged himself and his converts from the alleged contamination, that de Nobili was able to stay the tumult and avert disaster. The oath of purgation furnishes telling evidence of the straits in which the new missionary-method involved its author, and the lengths to which he was obliged to go:

> "I am no Parangi," so the oath ran, "I was not born on their soil nor am I allied to their race. In this God is my witness, and if I lie, I am willing not only to be deemed a traitor to God, and to be given over to the pains of hell hereafter, but also to suffer every conceivable chastisement in this world. I was born in Rome. My family are of the rank of noble rajahs in this country. . . . The holy spiritual law which I proclaim does not oblige a man to renounce his caste. . . . This law which I proclaim has been preached in

this very land by other men, Sannyasis and Saints alike. Whoever says this law is peculiar to the Paravans or Parangis lies: for since God is Lord of all castes, His law must likewise be observed by all."

This solemn declaration had the desired effect, and the storm was stayed.

Most serious, however, of all de Nobili's troubles was his conflict with his own ecclesiastical authorities. From Father Fernandez reports reached the Provincial of the Jesuit Order in Malabar, of the extremely strange and novel lines on which de Nobili was working, and the "monstrous mixture of Christianity and idolatry" which he was presenting to the heathen as the holy Christian religion. Alarm was taken, and de Nobili was summoned to Cochin to justify his policy and defend his strange "rites." This was the beginning of a controversy which lasted more than a decade, and involved the suspension of de Nobili's work at Madura for all that time. From Madura to Cochin, from Cochin to Goa, and from Goa to Rome the controversy was carried, de Nobili at each stage gaining a decisive victory over his opponents: and when, finally, in 1623, Pope Gregory XV. issued his famous bull, the Madura missionary and his methods were completely vindicated.

"Brahmans," declared the Pope, "are kept from confession of Christ, by difficulties about the cord and the Kudumi. Desiring to procure the conversion of these nations, after suitable discussion, we accord to the Brahmans and other Gentiles the cord, and the Kudumi, sandal paste, and purification of the body. These should not be received in idol temples, but only from priests after they have blessed them."

It was a dearly bought victory which de Nobili obtained. So far as concerned the most cherished desire of his heart, the winning of the Brahmans to Christianity under the guise of a higher Hinduism—that was ended. The long controversy had made all too plain the intimate connection of de Nobili with the Portuguese Christians of Goa, and henceforward the ears of the high caste men of Madura were closed to his most silvery words. But if the missionary's greatest dream was shattered, he quickly dreamed anew. The highest castes might indeed be unapproachable, yet there were still caste-men in abundance throughout the land, for whose adhesion he might hope: and fortified as he now was by the express authority of the Pope for the use of the "Madura methods," he would be free from any risk of interference by the local authorities of the Roman Church. So from 1624 there commenced a new period in de Nobili's life, and a new activity in which the role of recluse was exchanged for that of a wandering religious pilgrim. Clad in the orthodox yellow robe of a Brahman *Guru,* his head swathed in a turban, his feet protected by sandals, and carrying in his hand a pilgrim's long staff, the devoted Jesuit journeyed up and down the country, year in, year out, visiting places so far remote as Trichinopoly and Salem, preaching his gospel of compromise and enduring constant hardship. Many other like-minded priests joined him from time to time, and the "Roman Brahmans" became familiar figures in many a South-Indian town and village. Churches for their numerous followers sprang up in many places, for baptisms were frequent. Not many converts, it would appear, were drawn from the Brahmans, but the less important castes and the non-caste communities are reported to have yielded their thousands. . . .

For forty-two years de Nobili lived this life: a life of daily hardship, sacrifice and voluntary humiliation, such as has been seldom paralleled. At the end of that long period, now half-blind and quite broken down by reason of his labours and privations, the old man withdrew to Ceylon, but he could not remain out of his beloved India. In a little while he crossed the straits again, and journeyed to Mailapur to spend the evening of his days near the holy shrine of St. Thomas. Total blindness now overtook him, and in a rude mud hut he lingered for a few more years, but his austerities were rigorous as ever, and his literary activities continued unabated. Four Brahman secretaries were his constant attendants, and a touching picture has been preserved of their tender devotion in carrying the "Holy Father" every day to the adjoining church for prayer. On February 16, 1656, the end came, when, having reached his eightieth year, this apostle of India, second to none in single-hearted devotedness to his ideal, passed to his rest. Nearly one hundred thousand converts have been attributed to him, directly or indirectly, and allowing for much exaggeration their number must have been very great. . . .

De Nobili died, but his work lived on: and, by like-minded successors the system he had devised was continued and developed. . . . The highest point was reached under the third of the great triad of Madura Jesuits, *Father Joseph Beschi,* an Italian priest who reached India in 1707. Beschi adhered to the policy of the "Roman Brahmans," but in his missionary practice differed considerably from his predecessors. . . . If Hinduism has its ascetics, it has also its high priests who live in luxurious comfort, and whose outward surroundings are marked by pomp and circumstance. This was the line chosen by Beschi: by magnificence he would dazzle the people. When he travelled it was in a costly palanquin. In advance went an attendant bearing an umbrella of purple silk, at each side ran servants with gorgeous fans of peacock's feathers, and in the palanquin, upon a splendid tiger-skin and clad in rich and picturesque robes, reclined the mighty Guru! But Beschi was no empty-headed *poseur*. His method was adopted with a full understanding of the people and with many it worked well. Nor does his fame rest on these extravagances: it is based upon his wonderful scholarship. A born linguist, he attained so complete a mastery over Tamil that he became the ablest Tamil scholar of his time. No native scholar was hs equal. "High" Tamil as well as "Low," the Tamil of the scholarly Brahman as well as the colloquial language of the people, were equally familiar to Beschi. Dictionaries, grammars, works in poetry, and treatises in prose issued from his busy pen, which are read and valued to the present day. When first issued they delighted the native world of Southern India. So charmed with his learning was Chanda Sahib, the Nabob of Vellore, that he appointed him to high office in the State, and for his support presented him with four villages in the Trichinopoly district, which brought in a yearly revenue of 12,000 rupees.

3 / TESTING THE STRENGTH OF THE NEW CHRISTIANITY

The most meteoric course which Christianity has ever traversed is that which is followed in Japan at the end of the sixteenth and beginning of the seventeenth centuries. At first its missionaries found an open door to Japan because of the eagerness for Western trade and the wealth which that trade brought to any nobleman who could attract the Portuguese ships to his domains. The port of Nagasaki was actually given to the Jesuits to own and rule so that it might serve both as a haven for them and a center for the trade. The Japanese had a long tradition of accepting innovations from abroad, and the new religion spread rapidly through the southern part of the country, especially in Kyushu, the most westerly of the main islands and the natural point for European contact. Noblemen, who found the European emphasis upon discipline and honor congenial, were numbered among those baptized, though the great majority of the converts were from the lower classes. In a few years' time some 300,000 Japanese became Christians. Schools were established for training Japanese priests, and Christian painting and engraving were developed to a standard which won the admiration of foreigners.

But the growth was too rapid to avoid rousing the fears of the rulers of the country. Christianity's claims for absolute faith and allegiance were seen as undermining feudal law and order and as a possible threat to national unity. Forces of suppression were therefore put in operation, leading to a decline as rapid as the rise. It is this period of decline which has made Japanese Christianity most famous, for the infant Church had to face a persecution more severe than any that Christianity had known. Large numbers were burned at the stake, and when this proved ineffective in stamping out the faith, the most ingenious forms of death by torture were invented and applied. One young Japanese woman, for example, hung fourteen days head downward with slashed forehead in a pit without giving the sign of recantation before her death. Some five or six thousand became martyrs. The torture soon had the intended effect. Mass defections followed, and Christianity practically disappeared. Still, in order to keep it from reappearing, the government adopted the Closed Country Edict of 1636, which shut off Japan from all foreign contacts for over two centuries, and it long required the inhabitants of Nagasaki to trample on a cross every year.

The fact that such severe measures were necessary, and that despite them a noteworthy rebellion of Christians could take place in 1637-38 and in some out-of-the-way villages Christianity could survive secretly until the prohibitions were removed in the 1870s reveals a solid inner strength. Christianity was evidently no mere foreign importation.

The following selections include a contemporary description of one of the burnings, an example of the oaths of apostasy required of Christians leaving the faith, and the first part of the Closed Country Edict.

Persecution in Japan

The Martyrdom at Omura

. . . "Finally order came from Nagasaki, that all the Religious should be put to death, who so soone as they had understood the certainty thereof, shewed extraordinary signes of joy. Upon the 25 of August [1624] they were led forth of prison all five, fast bound, with ropes about their necks, and accompanied with a band of soldiers. The Priests went each bearing a crosse in his hand, and continually fixed in prayers till such time as they came to shippe, whither they entered with some few of the officers, the rest continuing their journey by land. They arrived at the

From C. R. Boxer, *The Christian Century in Japan, 1549-1650* (Berkeley: University of California Press; London: Cambridge University Press, 1951), pp. 436-37, 441-42, 439-40. Reprinted by permission of University of California Press.

place appointed for their death, a field called Hokonohara, when giving thanks unto those who had conducted them, for the pains they had taken they went to land, and the Priests lifting on high the crosses which they bare in their hands, they began to recite psalms with a loud voice; when Father *Carvalho* perceiving now a great multitude to be assembled, turning unto them, *you must understand,* said he, *that we are Christians, and that we die of our free and voluntary accord, for the faith of Christ our Lord.* The admirable serenity of their countenances put their joy so clearly in view of the beholders, that amazed thereat they said, *these men seemed to go rather to some feast or banquet, than unto death.* Finally, their desired end approaching, the first who was tied unto a stake, was Father Miguel Carvalho, of our *Society,* the second Father Peter *Vasquez,* of the Order of Saint *Dominicke,* the third, Father *Luis Sotelo,* the fourth Father *Luis Sasada* both of the same Order of *Saint Francis.* The fifth, Brother *Luis,* Observant of the third Order, a *Japanese;* Being ranked in this order, they were bound in such sort that after the cords should be burned, they might yet be able to stirre themselves to the end their troubled action and disordered motion, might incite the people to laughter. Every one was attired in his own habit, with his eyes fixed upon heaven. When the fire was kindled, which in regard of the small quantity of wood, burned very slowly, so that, the rope wherewith Brother *Luis* the Japanese was bound, being consumed, he might have departed at his pleasure. The rest of his valorous associates were jointly with loud voice reciting a certain devote prayer, and the fire grew to advance itself; when he departing from his stake, with noble contempt of those raging flames, made haste to do reverence, and kiss submissively the hands of the Priests his companions; then exhorting with a loud voice the standers by to embrace the faith of *Christ* in which alone is true safety and salvation, he returned generously unto the stake again, and leaning himself unto it, without any further tying (for he was already sufficiently bound in the bands of charity to *Christ* our Lord) he endured, without ever moving himself, the fury of those flames, until at length he rendered his invincible soul to God.

Oath of Apostasy

We have been Christian believers for many years. Yet we have found out that the Christian religion is an evil religion. It regards the next life as the most important. The threat of excommunication is held over those who disobey the padres' orders, whilst they are likewise kept from associating with the rest of humanity in the present world and doomed to be cast into Hell in the next. It further teaches that there is no salvation in the next life unless sinners confess their faults to the padres and receive their absolution. In this way, the people were led to place their trust in the padres. Yet all this was done with the design of taking the lands of others. When we learned this, I became an adherent of the Hokke sect and my wife of the Ikko sect.

We hereby witness this statement in writing before you, worshipful magistrate. Hereafter we shall never revoke our apostasy, not even in the secret places of the heart. Should we even entertain the slightest thought thereof, then let us be punished by God the Father, God the Son, and God the Holy Ghost, St. Mary, and all Angels and Saints. Let us forfeit all God's mercy, and all hope like Judas Iscariot, becoming a laughing-stock to all men, without thereby arousing the slightest pity, and finally die a violent death and suffer the torments of Hell without hope of salvation. This is our Christian Oath.

We tell you frankly that we have no belief whatsoever in Christianity in our hearts. Should we be guilty of any falsehood in this respect, now or in the future, then let each and both of us divinely punished by Bonten, Taishaku, Shiten-daijo, the great and small deities of the sixty and more provinces of Japan, particularly Gongen and Mishima-daimyojin of the two regions of Idzu and Hakone, Hachiman-daibosatsu, Tenman-daijizai-Tenjin, especially our own tutelary deity Suwa-daimyo-jin, and all the minor deities. This is our formal oath.
Second year of Shoho [1645].

KYUSUKE, HIS WIFE

[ENDORSEMENT]
The custom of recanting the Christian religion by such a formal oath, and of stamping on a holy image and so forth, has never yet been applied against the Christians in any other land. How can anyone who is troubled by their apostasy revoke it under these circumstances! Moreover, a true revocation of apostasy is quite impossible without the mediation of a padre. A secret revocation is not possible.

The apostate foreign padre—CHUAN
The apostate Japanese padres—RYOJUN

RYOHAKU

COUNTERSIGNED
We hereby certify that the above-mentioned Kyusuke and his wife have become members of the Ikko sect.

Saishoji Temple
Head Priest, SHUSAN

The Closed Country Edict

1. No Japanese ships may leave for foreign countries.
2. No Japanese may go abroad secretly. If anybody tries to do this, he will be killed, and the ship and owner(s) will be placed under arrest whilst higher authority is informed.
3. Any Japanese now living abroad who tries to return to Japan will be put to death.
4. If any Kirishitan [Christian] believer is discovered, you two [Nagasaki governors] will make a full investigation.
5. Any informer(s) revealing the whereabouts of a bateren [priest] will be paid 200 or 300 pieces of silver. If any other categories of Kirishitans are discovered, the informer(s) will be paid at your discretion as hitherto.
6. On the arrival of foreign ships, arrangements will be made to have them guarded by ships provided by the Omura clan whilst report is being made to Yedo, as hitherto.
7. Any foreigners who help the bateren or other criminal foreigners will be imprisoned at Omura as hitherto.
8. Strict search will be made for bateren on all incoming ships.
9. No offspring of Southern Barbarians [Europeans] will be allowed to remain. Anyone violating this order will be killed, and all relatives punished according to the gravity of the offence.
10. If any Japanese have adopted the offspring of Southern Barbarians they deserve to die. Nevertheless, such adopted children and their foster-parents will be handed over to the Southern Barbarians for deportation.
11. If any deportees should try to return or to communicate with Japan by letter or otherwise, they will of course be killed if they are caught, whilst their relatives will be severely dealt with, according to the gravity of the offence.

4 / WESTERN DOMINATION IN "ASIA'S ONLY CHRISTIAN COUNTRY"

In sharp contrast to the persecutions suffered by Christianity in Japan stands the easy acceptance of Christianity in the Philippines. In contrast, too, to the radical innovations in China and South India and the self-assurance of the Church in Japan stands the Western orientation and total dependence on Western leadership which characterized Philippine Christianity.

From the very first European contact the Filipinos seem to have been open to the new faith. In this they resembled animistic inhabitants of other island groups. When Magellan arrived in 1521 on his way around the world, the first Filipino king whom he visited accepted baptism along with eight hundred of his subjects. The Spanish conquest of the islands following the expedition of 1564 was accomplished with ease, and the people accepted Christianity so rapidly that by 1605 the majority were Christian. The work of conversion was accomplished by missionaries sent out by the various religious orders. So rapid a Christianization was naturally under suspicion of being superficial. Therefore, the Church had to address itself to the long task of deepening faith and increasing religious knowledge. For this the second generation of missionaries settled down to a prolonged occupation of the country which was to continue for three hundred years.

In some areas the monks and friars not only provided Christian leadership but also served as the pioneers of settled, agricultural life among a nomadic and untamed people. This was true among the Visayans, the inhabitants of the central islands of the archipelago. In other areas, as among the Tagalogs around Manila, the missionaries lived in fairly settled circumstances and in relative comfort. It was the work of these missionaries from Spain which was primarily responsible for both the strengths and the weaknesses which have been exhibited by Philippine Christianity. The following account gives a taste of their life and their methods of operation in both the wilder Visayan regions and the more settled Tagalog area.

Missionary Life in the Philippines

An intimate glimpse into the daily life and labors of . . . [the second generation of missionaries] is vouchsafed us by a precious document of 1660. It is a long letter written by Ignacio Alcina, a veteran of the Visayan missions. . . .

Each father has under his care at least two towns; some have three, others four and even five. I myself, this Lent of 1660, visited and heard confessions in four. Thus we are always on the move, carrying our houses on our backs like the tortoise, for wherever the missionary goes he must bring with him his domestic effects, and in many places his church equipment too. . . .

For the most part there is nothing in the towns except the priest's house and

From H. de la Costa, S.J., *The Jesuits in the Philippines, 1581-1768* (Cambridge, Mass.: Harvard University Press, 1961), pp. 458-59, 461-62, 469, 471-72, 475, 479-80. © 1961 by The President and Fellows of Harvard College. Reprinted by permission of the publisher.

the chapel, small or big according to the number of people, and a few huts which the natives use when they come to town. This they do only when the father is there, and they do not come every day but only on Sundays. The only ones who stay are the boys who are still learning their catechism, for we insist on their being there as long as the father is; the old folks too and the sick stay for a while. But even this much requires a great deal of persuasion, for they are scattered all over the countryside, wherever they have a mind to dwell. There they make the clearing from which they derive their sustenance, for they have neither store nor barn to draw on save forest and stream and their little rice field. Even the rice lasts them for only a small part of the year; the rest of the time most people manage with edible roots and leaves and an occasional fish or wild pig when they can catch it, for there is nowhere to buy these things even if they wanted to. These clearings are some of them two leagues, others three, four, five, and six leagues from the town; few are any closer, for the Visayans have no love for town life. Thus it takes them a day or more to come to town, and if the weather is bad and the seas rough they cannot come at all. When they come they must bring their food, pots to cook it in and plates to eat it out of, for there is nothing to be had in the town but weeds. . . . Most of the people do not even bother to go to their town huts, but proceed directly from their canoes to the church, both men and women, and from church back to them again, so that Sunday Mass over not a soul is left in town. . . .

. . . The fathers meet in their central residence four times a year, twice for a period of eight days and twice for fifteen. At these times they perform their religious duties and devote themselves exclusively to their personal sanctification [*a lo formal de la religión*]. During the rest of the year each one takes care of his stations and the spiritual needs of his communities, having recourse to the superior in all cases of special importance or difficulty. The missionary is by himself in his station, and so is all things to all men, and bears in himself the reputation of the entire order. This means that he must be a man of prayer, for here it is difficult to live as one ought without great intimacy with God. . . .

The stipend allowed each missionary by the government at this time was 100 pesos and 100 fanegas of hulled rice yearly for every 500 families or "tributes" in his area. Out of this stipend the superior of the residence gave to the missionary, as needed, provisions for himself and the four companions he usually took with him on his mission tours: two sacristans and two domestics. Out of it also came the money to buy equipment for houses, chapels, and portable Mass kits. But by far the biggest item of expenditure in the missionary's operating budget was the food and wages of the oarsmen or pack carriers without whom he could not go on the road at all. . . .

Alcina's observation that the Jesuits engaged in the ministry among the Tagalogs had a much easier time of it than those in the Visayas is true as far as living conditions and travel were concerned. The population was more settled and more prosperous; the towns and villages were closer together; travel was mostly by land; the capital of the colony was within easy reach. For this reason towns like Antipolo, Taytay, and Silang, which began as missions just as much as Dulag and Loboc, developed much more rapidly, and were now almost indistinguishable from parishes. . . .

Sanvítores [a noted Jesuit leader], assigned to the task [of conducting a popular mission in Tagalog country], prepared for it by an intensive study of Tagalog at Taytay, in the course of which he translated Jerónimo López's famous *acto de contrición*. López had found in the course of giving innumerable missions to the simple folk of the Spanish countryside that one of the most effective means of drawing them to a better life was to march through the streets of a town or village carrying a crucifix and crying out the act of contrition in a loud voice, varying this with short extempore ejaculations expressive of sorrow for sin, and wherever a crowd collected, at street corners or in the squares, expanding the formula into passionate exhortations to repentance. Usually people who merely stopped to stare stayed to pray, and soon the missioner was being followed by a vast procession singing hymns and shouting the act of contrition with him, often with sobs and tears. He led them in this manner to the church. where, after a brief instruction on how to make a good confession, he sent them to the priests waiting in the confessionals.

Sanvítores and his companion, Tomás de Andrade, set out on their mission tour late in 1662. They spent the advent season of that year and the lenten season of 1663 working their way from cattle ranch to cattle ranch east of Manila, making a sweep through the Aeta town of Santa Inés, a dependency of the Antipolo residence, and going as far as Maralaya Mountain near the Lake of Bai. The tour was a triumphant success. Not only did they bring many old and hardened sinners to repentance, but at Santa Inés pagan Aetas who had come down from the hills stayed to begin their catachumenate. The most spectacular mission, however, was that at the foot of Maralaya; for Maralaya was the hideout of a large band of outlaws and of others who owed money to the Spanish treasury or their heads to Spanish justice. The government seems to have guaranteed immunity from arrest to those who came to hear the missioners, for they came down in large numbers accompanied by their women and children. The two missioners had their hands happily full hearing confessions, solemnizing marriages, and teaching cat-echism to children as untutored as the wild creatures of the forest among which they were born. After the mission this strange community melted back into the jungle out of reach of the law, although the missioners were able to persuade many whose lives were not forfeit to return to the more settled if less exciting life of the ordinary taxpayer. . . .

In an account of the Tagalog parishes of this period it would not be fair to pass over in silence certain documents in which a number of abuses are laid at the door of the parish clergy by the civil authorities. Ex-Governor Corcuera, for instance, in returning to the Council of the Indies a report on the state of the Church in the Philippines which had been referred to him for comment, observed that the report failed to stress two outstanding abuses, namely, the practice of parish priests hav-ing the sick brought to the church for the last sacraments instead of their bringing the sacraments to the sick, as they were in duty bound, and the exorbitant stole fees charged in some parishes for marriages and funerals. He was careful to state that these abuses were by no means universal; nevertheless they existed, and were sufficiently widespread to require some appropriate action by the central government. . . .

The other abuses listed by Gómez de Espinosa [a government official] fall under three main headings: obligatory contributions, forced labor, and corporal punishment. Under the first heading may be classed the *pasalamat* (literally, thank-offering), which must have been originally a gift of rice brought by the people to their priest at harvest time, but which, according to Gómez de Espinosa, had degenerated in his time to the priest planting himself at the door of the church and telling the farmers as they came out how big a "gift" was expected of them. Other contributions similarly enforced were those to defray the expenses of the town fiesta, and to construct or repair parish buildings, churches, monu-ments, and so on. Under the heading of forced labor, Gómez de Espinosa enumerates the drafting of rowers and carriers when the priest went on a journey, the appointment of young men to a stated number of days or weeks of work in the mission compound, the custom of giving the girls of the village the task of keeping the church clean and the women that of furnishing the sacristy with linen and keeping the vestments in repair. Finally, Gómez de Espinosa objected to some of the forms of corporal punishment inflicted by some parish priests or by their fiscales, such as heavy beatings, the cutting off of women's hair, and the use of stocks and cangues.

For a parish priest to get his people to contribute to the expenses of the parish or to share in its common tasks is not in itself an abuse. By doing so, he is merely urging on them their ordinary obligation as Catholics. Nor, in fairness to Gómez de Espinosa, does he anywhere suggest that he thought otherwise. What he considered objectionable was that some parish priests urged the obligation in a manner difficult to distinguish from extortion. . . .

The question of inflicting corporal punishment for breaches of divine or ecclesiastical law is more of a problem, whose elucidation is better left to Fray Alonso Sandín. In a printed pamphlet of his published in 1685, he had this to say:

> It is true that there are parish priests who punish them [the natives] corporally when the need arises. They do so for the most part as fathers, and in matters which pertain to their spiritual welfare, for otherwise they would neither attend Mass of obligation, nor come to confession, nor perform their other Christian duties. This is because they pay little heed to reprimands, and would pay no heed whatever if they did not fear a moderate amount of corporal punishment. They are not, however, perturbed by such punishments, as long as they are within reason; for, although they are of limited intelligence, they know enough not to resent being punished if they deserve it; indeed they will freely admit that the father is quite right to punish them. Everyone who has any understanding of the native character considers these punishments to be absolutely necessary, otherwise they would hardly be Christians at all; as it is, they are preserved from committing many faults . . . I doubt not but there are some parish priests who punish immoderately. But you may be sure that if he has no influence with the alcalde mayor, he will be pulled up short at the least complaint of the native. However, this is also true, that if parish priest and alcalde mayor are of one mind, and if they are not zealous for the honor of God, then the native has no choice but to suffer in silence, or join the pagans in the hills.

5 / THE CONSERVATISM OF ASIA'S OLDEST PROTESTANT CHURCH

Protestantism had almost no part in the development of non-western Christianity during the sixteenth and seventeenth centuries. Not until the eighteenth century did the first regular Protestant missionaries begin to appear in Asia and Africa. Bartholomew Ziegenbalg, the Protestant pioneer in India, arrived there in 1708 under the auspices of the Danish mission which continued to work with some strength during most of that century.

In one part of Asia Protestantism got an earlier foothold not because of its own missionary labors but because it appropriated the results of

Roman Catholic work. The area was that of the Moluccas, or "Spice Islands," where the Portuguese had early penetrated in order to control the spice trade. The Portuguese established their domination over the area, and those inhabitants who were not Muslims soon became Christians. Then, in 1605, the Dutch threw the Portuguese out of the islands and captured the principal city of Amboina (from which the people of the area are known as Amboinese). The churches which the Catholics had erected were divested of their images, and the people who had been faithful Catholics overnight became faithful Protestants.

A highly conservative form of Christian life was established which changed little over the centuries. Christianity continued to identify itself with Dutch rule until 1950, when it became involved in a rebellion against the newly independent government of Indonesia. After that its outlook began to change. The description which follows is one written by a missionary observer who made a study of the islands in 1930, but his analysis of the attitudes of the Amboinese Christians and the relation of their church life to their traditional life could have been penned generations earlier.

The Christian Style of Life in the Spice Islands

The Amboinese, especially the Amboinese Christians, are a curious people. This tiny island, with its still primitive social organization which either perpetuates or preserves in a rudimentary form many features of the simplest social patterns at present known to us, has become the main cultural centre of the entire Moluccan archipelago, from Northern New Guinea down to the "South," i.e. Timor and the surrounding islands. Their history having been so closely intertwined with the Dutch, the Amboinese have embraced Christianity and in consequence have become the main culture bearers of the Moluccas. The fact that they are Christians, as a result of which they became intimately related to Dutch rule and received careful attention in religious and intellectual (schools) respect, is fundamental to their central position and to the prestige which they undoubtedly enjoy among the various primitive populations of the Moluccan islands by virtue of their being the most intelligible interpreters and representatives of the inevitable Western impact. . . . Because of all this the Amboinese Christians acquired a strong and sensitive sense of dignity, even enhanced by the fact that during the last 60 years they came to provide a considerable proportion of the Netherlands Indies

From Hendrik Kraemer, *From Missionfield to Independent Church. Report on a Decisive Decade in the Growth of Indigenous Churches in Indonesia* (London: SCM Press Ltd., 1958), pp. 13-17, 18-22. Reprinted by permission of the SCM Press Ltd. and Boekencentrum N.V. (Netherlands).

army. . . . They feel at least half European and they want to be Europeans. . . . All those peoples and tribes of the Indies which rebelled with armed force or which had to be subdued by the sword they consider "their enemies," just like the average Dutchman.

The economic aspects of the situation in Amboina are far from encouraging. . . . It is a great joy to sail through the Moluccas, because of the luxurious vegetation and the dazzling tropical splendour of sun, sea and land. The proverbial mildness of the tropics immediately strikes the eye. The Alfurs living on these islands are, however, especially endowed with a tropical carelessness and lack of wants, the two factors which always put to shame our entire European economic science with its arsenal of unconscious moral, psychological and climatological presuppositions. Hence they fall even more easily than other Indonesian peoples prey to other races who are more commercial-minded and more calculating. Of course there are some differences. The Amboinese Mohammedans are decidedly more industrious than their Christian fellow-countrymen, and somewhat more prosperous.

The historical causes of the extra laziness of Amboinese Christians have already been indicated in the general remarks which I made in the introduction to this section of my report. The fact that they are Christians and consequently consider themselves half European and the excessive care which in the course of centuries the government, as it appears now, has bestowed on the Amboinese Christians, have fostered a feeling of superiority in them. This feeling of superiority is not a result of Christianity, as harsh critics hastily want us to believe, but it is an *attendant phenomenon*. This phenomenon has two root causes: the political use which the government has always made of the Amboinese being Christians, and the typically Oriental conclusion which is drawn from this feeling of superiority, viz. a superior does not work, but lives from the labour of others. This is the curse of many Oriental societies, large or small. . . .

A few remarks on the moral and religious aspect should follow here, again in order to clarify the different condition. . . . The Amboinese in general are quite religious. i.e. religious in the sense of devoted to the Church. The Church is the institution commanding their loyalty. The Church buildings are the pride of the Amboinese *negorij* [village] dwellers. Hence so many beautiful churches can be seen. The poor Amboinese do not think it too much to build a beautiful church costing f20.000.—in a *negorij* such as Batugantung which numbers 1381 souls. This is possible in such a poor *negorij* because construction work is done in service to the *negorij,* because money is borrowed from other congregations, because people are willing to suffer hardships for its sake during long periods, and because everyone, including the fellow *negorij* dwellers who have emigrated to distant parts, is asked to make a contribution which is readily given on account of the community feeling. On Sundays the churches in the *negorijs* are full. They are truly peaceful village parishes. On closer analysis, this great attachment to the church is not pure religiosity only. In my opinion we could best say that local patriotism, inherent in these primitive communities, has become allied to the church with all its forms and laws, so that to their feeling, church and community are an inseparable entity. Hence, the Amboinese are also ardent Protestants, without being able to understand its true significance. They, as well as other inhabitants of the Moluccas who are under their spiritual guidance, consequently speak of the *agama Srani* (Protestantism) or *agama Ambon* (religion of Amboina), when they wish to contrast it to Roman Catholicism. Protestantism is *their* religion, their national palladium par excellence, and therefore they are strongly anti-Catholic and anti-Adventist, those two spiritual phenomena which have recently emerged on their spiritual horizon. The *agama,* the Church. has been completely incorporated into the old notion that whatever constituted the spiritual domain of the *orang tua-tua* (the ancestors) should also constitute theirs. The individual religious element of faithfulness to Christ and to the Gospel for its own sake is as yet practically unheard of, because their thinking is still collective. Moreover, they consider the *agama* their uniting link, and so the feelings expressed on this subject are often analogous to the utterances I usually hear in the Mohammedan world. . . . This is also the reason why it sometimes happens that, e.g., Chinese who on Sunday wish to worship in the great church in the city of Amboina are sent away at the door with the argument that this is a church of Amboinese—astonishing behaviour from a Christian viewpoint. The purely individual and at the same time universal quality of the Gospel remains a mystery not yet fathomed by the Amboinese generally. Therefore, their religion dissolves into much formalism as a matter of course. This may be seen from the strict segregation of classes; the smallest difference of status is observed and visibly demonstrated in the church on Sundays by means of differences in costume. This custom is considerably declining owing to the strong levelling process of recent times, but its underlying mentality is still quite vigorous. Christianity in Amboina is a silent and deeprooted tradition. If this tradition is destroyed, probably Christianity will largely cease to exist as a vital force. *One future task, therefore seems to me to be not the destruction of this tradition, but deepening it and shaping it into a well-founded possession which has been critically purged and personally assimilated. In this connection the training of Indigenous teachers constitutes a problem of great significance, which can hardly be overrated.* Only then will Amboina begin to have an internal Church history, which is as yet not the case. At present Amboina merely has an external Church history.

Their tradition, the revered custom of the *orang tua-tua,* includes numerous pre-Christian remnants which express themselves in superstition, fear of ghosts, etc. Not everything in these practices is pre-Christian: they also contain elements which might be called the apprehension of Christianity of which they were capable by their disposition and by the degree of spiritual guidance which they received for centuries. I am here thinking of the Eucharist, which is treated as a mystery, causing awe and bringing salvation at the same time. It is shrouded in secrecy, the people prepare for it by fasting and *purification,* looking neither left nor right, they go to receive the Eucharist. After the service the elders go and distribute it among the sick who were unable to come. This phenomenon is, I think, misunderstood if we merely fight it, without realizing that in this way the Amboinese have stolen from Protestantism with its matter-of-fact atmosphere a religious satisfaction which should have been given to them in a normal and legitimate way through the Gospel. I am also thinking of their sense of the distinction between the profane and the holy, as seen in the custom which forbids prospective Church members to *dansi-dansi* and *menari* (dance) during their preparation, and this among the Amboinese who love dancing so much. In this case the people have created a little standard of their own, which we cannot shrug off without having understood its meaning. Missions and Christianization mean above all: digging channels for the expression of normal religious needs.

Amboina furnishes proof of the fact that cruel repression and obstinate neglect of former religious life without a search for the natural needs behind the frequently distorted forms which require fulfilment in the new religion, are best suited to keep superstition alive in a long-lived and most sterile way. . . . The Amboinese Christians were by edict prohibited to give thanks by means of burning candles in the church, or to accept a dowry, to perform the ritual lamentation for the dead, which consisted of tearing out their hair and weeping etc. . . . Seeing how much superstition still prevails, side by side with honest Christian behaviour and faithfulness to the Church, we do not feel inclined to admire this blind and yet systematic suppression, no matter how understandable it may have been in the light of those times. It was not education but an expression of destructive contempt.

6 / THE EIGHTEENTH-CENTURY STAGNATION OF ASIAN CHRISTIANITY

The vigor and expansiveness of the sixteenth and seventeenth centuries was followed by a period of depression and decline. The skepticism of the Enlightenment in Europe gradually reduced the interest in missionary work in Asia. In the latter half of the eighteenth century the stream of Catholic missionaries was reduced to a trickle, and Protestant reenforcements ceased altogether. The suppression of the Jesuit order robbed Asian Christianity of its most robust and creative elements. The final decision to reject the Chinese rites and the Malabar rites ended whatever tendency toward experimentation there had been.

In these circumstances church life in Asia became stagnant. One of the most sweeping criticisms of non-Western Christianity which has ever been penned comes to us from that period. It was written by the French Abbé J. A. Dubois, who served for a long period in India and thus knew what he was criticizing. He had a very low opinion of the Christianity of India and despaired completely of ever winning Indians to a true Christianity. Some of his criticisms were based on narrowly ethnocentric standards taken from the West, and consequently some of the objects of his attack can be taken as evidence that the Asian Christians were making Christianity their own and not just following Western patterns. But some of his criticisms, as will be seen, were more fundamental and place a question mark alongside many of the Christian successes that had been achieved in the earlier period.

Dubois belonged to the remnant that tried to fill the gaps left by the deported Jesuits. He wrote early in the nineteenth century when the tide had already begun to turn and new Protestant movements and new Catholic interest had begun to appear. But the situation he describes is that which prevailed before the new forces had been able to make themselves felt, and hence what he describes is more typical of the late eighteenth century.

The Foibles and Failures of Indian Christians

The greater, the by far greater number [of Indian Christians] exhibit nothing but a vain phantom, an empty shade of Christianity. In fact, during a period of twenty five years that I have familiarly conversed with them, lived among them as their religious teacher and spiritual guide, I would hardly dare to affirm that I have any where met a sincere and undisguised Christian.

In embracing the Christian religion, they very seldom heartily renounce their leading superstitions, towards which they always entertain a secret bent, which does not fail to manifest itself in the several occurrences of life; and in many circumstances where the precepts of their religion are found to be in opposition to their leading usages, they rarely scruple to overlook the former, and conform themselves to the latter.

Besides, in order to make true Christians among the natives, it would be necessary before all things, to erase from the code of the Christian religion, the great leading precept of *charity;* for try to persuade a Hindoo [i.e. Indian] that this religion places all men on equal footing in the sight of God, our common Maker and Father; that the being born in a high caste, authorizes nobody to look with indifference or contempt on the persons born in a lower tribe; that even the exalted Brahmin, after embracing Christianity, ought to look upon the humble pariah as his brother, and be ready to bestow upon him all marks of kindness and love in his power; try to prevail upon the christian Hindoo to forgive an often imaginary injury, such as would be that of being publicly upbraided with having violated any one of their vain usages; try to persuade even the low-born pariah, that after turning a Christian he ought for ever to renounce the childish distinction of *Right and Left Hand,* upon which he lays so much stress, and which he considers as the most honourable characteristic of his tribe; tell him that as that distinction of *Right and Left Hand* proves a source of continual quarrel, fighting, and animosity, it becomes wholly incompatible with the first duties imposed upon him by the Christian religion, and must altogether be laid aside; try to prevail upon parents, in opposition to the established customs, to permit a young widow, their daughter, who, on account of her youth, is exposed to dishonor both herself and family, to marry again; so to act

From Abbé J. A. Dubois, *Letters on the State of Christianity in India* (London: Longman, Hurst, Rees, Orme, Brown, and Green, 1823), pp. 63-65, 32-33, 68-70, 73-75.

in opposition to any of their leading usages and practices; your lectures, your instructions, your expostulations on such subjects, will be of no avail; and your Christians will continue to live the slaves of their Antichristian prejudices and customs. . . .

Being at Carricaul, about twenty-eight years ago, I preached on a Sunday to the assembled congregation a sermon in the *Tamul* language, on the divine origin of the christian religion. Among other topics to prove my subject, I insisted on the intrinsic weakness and inadequacy of the means employed in the establishment of this religion, generally hated and persecuted everywhere, quite destitute of all human support, and left to its own resources amidst every kind of contradictions. I several times repeated, in treating this topic, that the christian religion had for its founder *a peasant of Galilee, the son of a humble carpenter,* who took for his assistants twelve low born men, twelve ignorant and illiterate *fishermen.* These words *the son of a carpenter! twelve fishermen!* many times repeated, gave offence to my audience, which was entirely composed of native christians; and the sermon was no sooner finished than three or four of the principal among them came and informed me, that the whole congregation had been highly scandalized by hearing me apply to Christ the appellation of *the son of a carpenter,* and to his apostles that of *fishermen;* that I could not be ignorant that the castes both of carpenters and fishermen were two of the lowest and vilest in the country; that it was highly improper to attribute to Christ and his disciples so low and abject an origin; that if pagans, who sometimes come through motives of curiosity to their religion assemblies, heard such objectionable accounts of our religion, their contempt and hatred of it would be considerably increased, etc., etc. Finally, they advised me, if in future I had occasion to mention in my sermons the origin of Christ or his apostles, not to fail to say that both were born in the noble tribe of *kshatrys* or rajahs, and never to mention their low profession. . . .

Seeing the empire of the senses over these people, and that their imagination was only to be roused by strongly moving objects, the first missionaries among them judged that some advantage might result to the cause of religion by accommodating themselves, as far as possible, to their dispositions. Agreeably to this idea, the ordinary pomp and pageantry which attend the catholic worship, so objectionable to the protestant communions in general, were not judged by them striking enough to make a sufficient impression on the gross minds of the Hindoos. They in consequence incumbered the catholic worship with an additional superstructure of outward shew, unknown in Europe, which in many instances does not differ much from that prevailing among the gentiles, and which is far from proving a subject of edification to many a good and sincere Roman catholic.

This Hindoo pageantry is chiefly seen in the festivals celebrated by the native Christians. Their processions in the streets, always performed in the night time, have indeed been to me at all times a subject of shame. Accompanied with hundreds of *tom-toms* (small drums), trumpets, and all the discordant noisy music of the country; with numberless torches, and fire-works; the statue of the saint placed on a car which is charged with garlands of flowers, and other gaudy ornaments, according to the taste of the country—the car slowly dragged by a multitude shouting all along the march—the congregation surrounding the car all in confusion, several among them dancing, or playing with small sticks, or with naked swords: some wrestling, some playing the fool; all shouting, or conversing with each other, without any one exhibiting the least sign of respect or devotion. Such is the mode in which the Hindoo Christians in the inland country celebrate their festivals. They are celebrated, however, with a little more decency on the coast. They are all exceedingly pleased with such a mode of worship, and any thing short of such pageantry, such confusion and disorder, would not be liked by them. . . .

In order to give you a striking idea of the religious dispositions of the Hindoo, and as a strong instance of what I asserted above, that there was to be found among them, nothing else but a vain phantom of Christianity, without any real or practical faith, I will with shame and confusion quote the following scandalous instance.

When the late Tippoo Sultan sought to extend his own religious creed all over his dominions, and make by little and little all the inhabitants in Mysore converts to Islamism, he wished to begin this fanatical undertaking with the native Christians living in his country, as the most odious to him, on the score of their religion. In consequence, in the year 1784, he gave secret orders to his officers in the different districts, to make the most diligent inquiries after the places where Christians were to be found, and to cause the whole of them to be seized on the same day, and conducted under strong escorts to Seringapatam. This order was punctually carried into execution; very few of them escaped, and I have it from good authority, that the aggregated number of the persons seized in this manner, amounted to more than 60,000.

Some time after their arrival at Seringapatam, Tippoo ordered the whole to undergo the rites of circumcision, and be made converts to

Mahometanism. The Christians were put together during the several days that the ceremony lasted: and, oh shame!—oh scandal!—will it be believed in the Christian world?—no one, not a single individual among so many thousands, had courage enough to confess his faith under this trying circumstance, and become a martyr to his religion. The whole apostatized *en masse,* and without resistance, or protestations, tamely underwent the operation of circumcision; no one among them possessing resolution enough to say, "I am a Christian, and I will die rather than renounce my religion!"

So general a defection, so dastardly an apostacy, is, I believe, unexampled in the annals of Christianity.

After the fall of the late Tippoo Sultan, most of those apostates came back to be reconciled to their former religion, saying that their apostacy had been only external, and they always kept in their hearts the true faith in Christ. About 2,000 of them fell in my way, and nearly 20,000 returned to the Mangalore district, from whence they had been carried away, and rebuilt there their forcer places of worship. God preserve them all from being exposed in future to the same trials; for should this happen, I have every reason (notwithstanding their solemn protestations when again reconciled to Christianity) to apprehend the same sad results, that is to say, a tame submission, and a general apostacy.

III / THE NINETEENTH AND EARLY TWENTIETH CENTURIES: EXPANSION AND INVOLVEMENT

INTRODUCTION

With the end of the eighteenth century the non-Western world entered an entirely new phase of its long experience with Christianity. The change was marked first by an enormous increase in the amount of Christian activity. The Evangelical Revival in Europe and America resulted in the formation of numerous new missionary societies among the Protestants, starting in the 1790s in England and a decade or two later on the Continent and in America. Soon thereafter missionary interest began to grow again among the Roman Catholics of Europe, and many new societies and orders were founded for work in Asia and Africa. As a result of these revived efforts new churches appeared in many parts of those continents.

The new period was remarkable too for the domination of non-Western Christianity by the Western churches. This is understandable in light of the fact that the nineteenth and early twentieth centuries were the time of the greatest Western domination in world affairs. The self-assured independence of the East in earlier centuries was lost, and the reassertion of independence had not yet begun. Therefore, much of this section of our story is devoted to the work of Western Christians, though always with an eye to the way in which their work and the results of their work fitted into non-Western life. As will be seen, sometimes it fitted not at all but remained an alien imposition. At other times it was almost totally absorbed and lost much of its Christian identity. And occasionally it fitted in a creative and challenging way into its new environment.

A further new development of this period was the rise of social service as a form of Christian mission. The social work of Christianity became its most important feature for the non-Western world as a whole. The following selections deal, first, with the work of the Westerners and the way it fitted into non-Western life, second, with the non-Western variations of Christianity which arose and, finally, with the main developments of Christian social service.

NEW WESTERN MISSIONS AND NEW NON-WESTERN CHURCHES

7 / THE LIFE OF THE PIONEER MISSIONARY

The enthusiasm and devotion which marked the new mission interest in the West carried the missionaries not only to the principal lands where Christian work had been established during the previous centuries but also to new areas hitherto untouched by Christianity and perhaps untouched by the outside world at all. Paramount among these new areas was Africa. Through the sixteenth, seventeenth, and eighteenth centuries Western missionaries had passed by Africa with little concern for that continent. Asia was their goal. Some Roman Catholic work, as has been noted, was done along the west coast and on the lower Congo, and a little Protestant effort was exerted, mainly by the Moravians at the Cape, but these ventures proved to be without lasting results.

The nineteenth century saw a great change. A missionary interest in Africa sprang up, at first as a result of the growing concern about slavery and the slave trade. The French Cardinal Lavigerie, who was the protagonist of the antislavery crusade in Europe, was also the principal inaugurator of Catholic missions in Africa. Already, the same Englishmen who stirred the conscience of their country over slavery had taken an interest in initiating Protestant missions in Africa. The colony for freed slaves established in Sierra Leone late in the eighteenth century became a few years later the first center for African missions of the newly founded Church Missionary Society of the Anglican communion. The freed slaves themselves became agents of Christianization along the Guinea coast as far as Nigeria. Missionaries joined with these Christian Africans in opening up the interior of West Africa for Christianity.

A second route into the continent was opened up at about the same time. That was the route north from the Cape. Here the leading pioneer was not the Church Missionary Society but the London Missionary Society, a largely Congregational body. It too was committed to the fight against slavery along with the proclamation of the Gospel. This commitment brought it into constant difficulties with the white settlers of South Africa, and part of the reason for pressing north was to outflank the Boers who were pushing into the interior. A series of outstanding representatives of this Society—John Philip, Robert Moffat, and Moffat's son-in-law, David Livingstone—were involved in the struggle with the Boers and the push to the north. It was Livingstone who first broke a way through the Kalahari Desert and reached the more inviting lands further north. In doing so he formed the grand design of opening up the interior of Africa to "commerce and Christianity" and thus destroying the slave trade and bringing a fuller life to the people. For the remaining years of his life he pursued this goal.

The following passage, written by Livingstone in his first public report, shows the genesis of this dream and records something of the difficulties of his pioneer life. In its lines can be seen his antipathy for the Boers and his great appreciation for Africans. It also reveals how unconsciously and almost unintentionally the norms of Western Christianity were transferred to the new Christians of Africa.

Livingstone's Life as a Pioneer Missionary

The general instructions I received from the Directors of the London Missionary Society led me, as soon as I reached Kuruman or Lattakoo, then, as it is now, their farthest inland station from the Cape, to turn my attention to the north. Without waiting longer at Kuruman than was necessary to recruit the oxen, which were pretty well tired by the long journey from Algoa Bay, I proceeded, in company with another missionary, to the Bakuena or Bakwain country, and found Sechele, with his tribe, located at Shokuane. . . .

I was from the first struck by his intelligence, and by the marked manner in which we both felt drawn to each other. . . . As soon as he had an opportunity of learning, he set himself to read with such close application that, from being comparatively thin, the effect of having been fond of the chase, he became quite corpulent from want of exercise. Mr. Oswell gave him his first lesson in figures, and he acquired the alphabet on the first day of my residence at Chonuane. He was by no means an ordinary specimen of the people, for I never went into the town but I was pressed to hear him read some chapters of the Bible. . . .

Seeing me anxious that his people should believe the words of Christ, he once said, "Do you imagine these people will ever believe by your merely talking to them? I can make them do nothing except by thrashing them; and if you like, I shall call my head men, and with your litupa (whips of rhinoceros hide) we will soon make them believe together." The idea of using entreaty and persuasion to subjects to become Chris-

From David Livingstone, *Missionary Travels and Researches in South Africa* (New York: Harper & Row, Publishers, 1860), pp. 9, 16, 18-22, 35, 43, 92-94, 97, 105-6.

tians—whose opinion on no other matter would he condescend to ask—
was especially surprising to him. He considered that they ought only to be
too happy to embrace Christianity at his command. During the space
of two years and a half he continued to profess to his people his full
conviction of the truth of Christianity; and in all discussions on the subject he took that side, acting at the same time in an upright manner in
all the relations of life. He felt the difficulties of his situation long before
I did, and often said, "Oh, I wish you had come to this country before I
became entangled in the meshes of our customs!" In fact, he could not
get rid of his superfluous wives, without appearing to be ungrateful to
their parents, who had done so much for him in his adversity.

Sechele continued to make a consistent profession for about three
years; and perceiving at last some of the difficulties of his case, and also
feeling compassion for the poor women, who were by far the best of our
scholars, I had no desire that he should be in any hurry to make a full
profession by baptism, and putting away all his wives but one. His principal wife, too, was about the most unlikely subject in the tribe ever to
become any thing else than an out-and-out greasy disciple of the old
school. She has since become greatly altered, I hear, for the better; but
again and again have I seen Sechele send her out of church to put her
gown on, and away she would go with her lips shot out, the very picture
of unutterable disgust at his new-fangled notions.

When he at last applied for baptism, I simply asked him how he,
having the Bible in his hand, and able to read it, thought he ought to
act. He went home, gave each of his superfluous wives new clothing, and
all his own goods, which they had been accustomed to keep in their
huts for him, and sent them to their parents with an intimation that
he had no fault to find with them, but that in parting with them he
wished to follow the will of God. . . . Here commenced the opposition
which we had not previously experienced. All the friends of the di-
vorced wives became opponents of our religion. The attendance at school
and church diminished to very few besides the chief's own family. They
all treated us still with respectful kindness, but to Sechele himself they
said things which, as he often remarked, had they ventured on in former
times, would have cost them their lives. . . .

The place where we first settled with the Bakwains is called Chonuane, and it happened to be visited, during the first year of our residence
there, by one of those droughts which occur from time to time in even
the most favored districts of Africa.

The belief in the gift or power of rain-making is one of the most deeply-rooted articles of faith in this country. The chief Sechele was himself a noted rain-doctor, and believed in it implicitly. He has often assured me that he found it more difficult to give up his faith in that than in any thing else which Christianity required him to abjure. I pointed out to him that the only feasible way of watering the gardens was to select some good, never-failing river, make a canal, and irrigate the adjacent lands. This suggestion was immediately adopted, and soon the whole tribe was on the move to the Kolobeng, a stream about forty miles distant. The experiment succeeded admirably during the first year. The Bakwains made the canal and dam in exchange for my labor in assisting to build a square house for their chief. They also built their own school under my superintendence. Our house at the River Kolobeng, which gave a name to the settlement, was the third which I had reared with my own hands. A native smith taught me to weld iron; and having improved by scraps of information in that line from Mr. Moffat, and also in carpentering and gardening, I was becoming handy at almost any trade, besides doctoring and preaching; and as my wife could make candles, soap, and cloths, we came nearly up to what may be considered as indispensable in the accomplishments of a missionary family in Central Africa, namely, the husband to be a jack-of-all-trades without doors, and the wife a maid-of-all-work within. . . .

Another adverse influence with which the mission had to contend was the vicinity of the Boers of the Cashan Mountains. During that time no winter passed without one or two tribes in the East country being plundered of both cattle and children by the Boers. The plan pursued is the following: one or two friendly tribes are forced to accompany a party of mounted Boers, and these expeditions can be got up only in the winter, when horses may be used without danger of being lost by disease. When they reach the tribe to be attacked, the friendly natives are ranged in front, to form, as they say, "a shield"; the Boers then coolly fire over their heads till the devoted people flee and leave cattle, wives, and children to the captors. This was done in nine cases during my residence in the interior, and on no occasion was a drop of Boer's blood shed. News of these deeds spread quickly among the Bakwains, and letters were repeatedly sent by the Boers to Sechele, ordering him to come and surrender himself as their vassal, and stop English traders from proceeding into the country with fire-arms for sale. But the discovery of Lake Ngami, here-after to be described, made the traders come in fivefold greater numbers, and Sechele replied, "I was made an independent chief and placed here by God, and not by you. I was never conquered by

Mosilikatze, as those tribes whom you rule over; and the English are my friends. I get everything I wish from them. I can not hinder them from going where they like." . . .

[For the exploratory trip across the Kalahari Desert] one of the Bushmen, named Shobo, consented to be our guide. . . . Shobo gave us no hope of water in less than a month. Providentially, however, we came sooner than we expected to some supplies of rain-water in a chain of pools. It is impossible to convey an idea of the dreary scene on which we entered after leaving this spot: the only vegetation was a low scrub in deep sand; not a bird or insect enlivened the landscape. It was, without exception, the most uninviting prospect I ever beheld; and, to make matters worse, our guide Shobo wandered on the second day. We coaxed him on at night, but he went to all points of the compass on the trails of elephants which had been here in the rainy season, and then would sit down in the path, and in his broken Sichuana say, "No water, all country only; Shobo sleeps; he breaks down; country only"; and then coolly curl himself up and go to sleep. The oxen were terribly fatigued and thirsty; and on the morning of the fourth day, Shobo, after professing ignorance of every thing, vanished altogether. We went on in the direction in which we last saw him, and about eleven o'clock began to see birds; then the trail of a rhinoceros. At this we unyoked the oxen, and they, apparently knowing the sign, rushed to find the water in the River Mahabe, which comes from the Tamunak'le, and lay to the west of us. The supply of water in the wagons had been wasted by one of our servants, and by the afternoon only a small portion remained for the children. This was a bitterly anxious night; and next morning the less there was of water, the more thirsty the little rogues became. The idea of their perishing before our eyes was terrible. It would almost have been a relief to me to have been reproached with being the entire cause of the catastrophe; but not one syllable of upbraiding was uttered by their mother, though the fearful eye told the agony within. In the afternoon of the fifth day, to our inexpressible relief, some of the men returned with a supply of that fluid of which we had never before felt the true value.

The cattle, in rushing along to the water in the Mahabe, probably crossed a small patch of trees containing tsetse, an insect which was shortly to become a perfect pest to us. Shobo had found his way to the Bayeiye, and appeared, when we came up to the river, at the head of the party; and, as he wished to show his importance before his friends, he walked up boldly and commanded our whole cavalcade to stop, and to bring forth fire and tobacco, while he coolly sat down and smoked his pipe. It was such an inimitably natural way of showing off, that we all stopped to admire the acting, and, though he had left us previously in the lurch, we all liked Shobo, a fine specimen of that wonderful people, the Bushmen. . . .

The Makololo whom we met on the Chobe were delighted to see us; and as their chief Sebituane was about twenty miles down the river, Mr. Oswell and I proceeded in canoes to his temporary residence. He had come from the Barotse town of Naliele down to Sesheke as soon as he heard of white men being in search of him, and now came one hundred miles more to bid us welcome into his country. . . .

As we were the very first white men the inhabitants had ever seen, we were visited by prodigious numbers. Among the first who came to see us was a gentleman who appeared in a gaudy dressing-gown of printed calico. Many of the Makololo, besides, had garments of blue, green, and red baize, and also of printed cottons; on inquiry, we learned that these had been purchased, in exchange for boys, from a tribe called Mambari, which is situated near Bihe. This tribe began the slave-trade with Sebituane only in 1850. The Makololo declare they never heard of people being bought and sold till then, and disliked it, but the desire to possess the guns prevailed, and eight old guns were exchanged for as many boys; these were not their own children, but captives of the black races they had conquered. I have never known in Africa an instance of a parent selling his own offspring. . . .

In talking with my companions over these matters, the idea was suggested that, if the slave-market were supplied with articles of European manufacture by legitimate commerce, the trade in slaves would become impossible. It seemed more feasible to give the goods, for which the people now part with their servants, in exchange for ivory and other products of the country, and thus prevent the trade at the beginning, than to try to put a stop to it at any subsequent steps. This could only be effected by establishing a highway from the coast into the centre of the country.

As there was no hope of the Boers allowing the peaceable instruction of the natives at Kolobeng, I at once resolved to save my family from exposure to this unhealthy region by sending them to England, and to return alone, with a view to exploring the country in search of a healthy district that might prove a centre of civilization, and open up the interior by a path to either the east or west coast. This resolution led me down to the Cape in April, 1852, being the first time during eleven years that I had visited the scenes of civilization. . . .

8 / THE CIRCUMSTANCES OF CONVERSION

The spread of Christianity in the non-Western world in modern times has not usually followed the pattern set in Europe in medieval times. In Europe the conversion of a king or chieftain was normally the decisive point in the conversion of a country. The king's decision entailed the decision of his nobles and eventually that of the people as a whole. The modern movement into Christianity has generally taken place at a social level below that of kings and nobility and has not usually involved whole countries. Yet in certain parts of Africa and in most of the South Pacific islands the medieval pattern was resurrected. Khame of Bechuanaland and Ranovalona II of Madagascar were replicas of the medieval monarchs who led their subjects into the Christian faith.

In the South Pacific, Christian missionaries arrived just at the time when the introduction of firearms was bringing about the unification of small clan groups into larger kingdoms under the dominance of chieftains who could take the lead in Christianization. In this way Tahiti, Hawaii, Fiji, and Tonga became unified and eventually Christian kingdoms. Usually one missionary organization approached each kingdom or each island group, and all the people became members of one national church. Tahiti was the first to be approached and the first to become Christian, under the leadership of Pomare II. The Cook Islands, Hawaii, Samoa, and Tonga followed.

One of the most critical areas was Fiji. These islands contained a larger population and a more advanced culture than most of the other groups. The Methodist Missionary Society from Great Britain began work there in 1835. Fiji at that time was coming under the domination of one of its many small chiefdoms. The town of Bau was extending its influence over all the other towns through constant warfare. At its head was the vigorous and remorseless leader, Seru, who had been given the name of Thakombau, meaning "Bau is bad." Missionaries were able to settle in some of the Bauan dependencies and finally, after many requests, Joseph Waterhouse secured permission to live in Bau itself. This permission represented a considerable concession on the part of the King, for though there had been a number of conversions to Christianity in some of his towns, Thakombau had set his face against the teachings of the new faith and had declared he would never forsake his ferocious ways.

However, at the beginning of 1854 the situation changed rapidly. Thakombau was beset by a widespread rebellion in his domains and danger from the ancient power of Rewa. His attacks on rebel strongholds were repulsed, and it was widely believed that his power was on the decline. In this situation he began to look with more interest on the teaching of the missionary and to doubt his ancestral deities. The following report, written by Mr. Waterhouse, reveals some of the forces which were operative in his conversion and doubtless in the conversion of other kings or chiefs who became Christians.

The Time of Decision in Fiji

It was on the 24th of April [1854] that the fleet returned to Bau from Sawakasa. The mind of the king was strangely agitated. All seemed lost. It seemed that his enemies must soon conquer him, and that the missionaries were his only friends. On entering his house he found the following letter:

To THAKOMBAU—I write to make known my love to you and the Bauan friends. When I arrived in Sydney, I received a letter which concerns you and the people of Bau. The letter is the writing of the consul at Rewa; and I hear that a letter has been sent to Great Britain, and another to America; and I am not certain whether Fiji will be in danger, or whether it will escape; for the consul's letter is a bad one. He says, you commanded the property of the white people to be burnt.

I expect to visit you with the Tongan friends to bring away my canoe; and when we have finished planting, we shall come to you. It is good, Thakombau, that you should consider the thing which concerns the white people; and when the Fiji friends wish to do their minds, do not be guided by them. It is good you should be humble; it will be well for you and your land. I wish, Thakombau, you would *lotu* [become Christian]. When I visit you, we will talk about it; for I desire that Bau and Fiji friends may stand well. But it will be well for you, Thakombau, to think wisely in these days. This is the end of my writing.

I, George Tubou. [King of the Tonga Islands]

The king of Tonga, having visited the colony of New South Wales, had returned to his dominions deeply impressed with the necessity of accelerating the civilization of Tonga and Fiji; and dispatched a canoe with the above letter to the Bauan king. . . .

The politicians of Fiji were anxiously observing the state of Somo-

From Joseph Waterhouse, *The King and People of Fiji: Containing a Life of Thakombau: With Notices of the Fijians, Their Manners, Customs and Superstitions Previous to the Great Religious Reformation in 1854* (London: Wesleyan Conference Office, 1866), pp. 243-44, 253-59, 261, 270-72.

somo [a strongly anti-Christian principality.] They had noticed that in the case of Rewa, soon after the withdrawal of the missionaries, that city had been destroyed. They attributed its destruction to its refusal to embrace Christianity, and the subsequent departure of the religious teachers. . . . The city politicians, and Thakombau himself, began to think that Somosomo had rejected Christianity, without any degree of punishment being visibly attached to the present generation. This was the point that they were concerned to know.

The commencement of 1854 solved this problem. One midnight three conspirators stealthily entered Tui Cakau's [ruler of Somosomo] house. One of them gently lifted up the mosquito-curtain, when the house lamp revealed the position of the unsuspecting victim. The other two ruffians clubbed the sleeping chief. It is said that he awoke, and inquired, "Will you kill me?" The reply was, "Sir, the moon sets to-night." A well-directed blow with a battle-axe then finished his unfortunate career. His death was a signal for a sanguinary civil war.

The politicians were alarmed. The fourteenth and fifteenth verses of the tenth of Matthew were again quoted. It was no mitigation that a missionary was now actually living at Bau, and could abandon them if they refused to hearken to his instruction. Doubtless this consideration weighed heavily with the king of Bau. He was the first to communicate the intelligence to the missionary. This he did with much solemnity. For a day he kept uttering, "Tui Cakau is dead!" . . .

The panic during the late attack on Kaba also made a deep impression on the mind of the king. The gods had been propitiated, and had promised him success. Yet he had never sustained a defeat so unaccountable. What if the words of his missionary be true? What if his former success has been the result of wisdom of his own plots, and the valour of his own followers? Then his past victories were not "of the gods," and he has been believing a lie. Why should he not embrace the truth, and become a Christian?

Then fell that well-directed shell which was thrown by him who so ably rules the Tonga group.

King George's letter arrived at the right moment. It presented to the king an opportunity of altering the national religion with credit to himself, and abundance of excuses to his followers. His cwn heart told him that the time for repentance and reformation had come. But the carnal mind is enmity against God; and he delayed.

His principal queen, Adi Sumanunu, now urged decision. Her efforts were ridiculed by the majority of the regal harem. "The queen wants to escape the strangling which will take place on the death of her lord," said some. Others asserted that "the queen knew that such was her influence over the king, that she would become his married wife; and that was the sole reason why she wished him to become a Christian." Amidst these galling remarks, the queen continued to side with the missionary.

On the 27th of April the missionary had an unusually long interview in private with the king, entreating him to take up his cross and renounce heathenism. As his past life was brought vividly before him, he wept silently before his faithful reprover. "Will not God cast me off, if I call upon His name whom I have so ill-treated?" was his inquiry. At length he resolved to make the venture; and briefly, in a spirit of meekness altogether novel to his character, announced his decision to the missionary, who bade farewell to the king with a heart excited with thankfulness and joy, striving to repress the misgivings he could not but feel, that, after all, this good promise might not be fulfilled. . . .

On Saturday Thakombau assembled his male relatives and the principal chiefs of the city. The political aspect of the question was fully discussed. A near relative of the king ventured to remind Thakombau, that he himself was the only man troubling Fiji; and that if he resolved to become a Christian, the whole country would rejoice. It was eventually resolved that the king and Ratu Mua should wait on the missionary, as a deputation, to make certain inquiries. The result of this interview was deemed satisfactory, and the deputation returned to the meeting, and made its report. It was then resolved that the religion of Christ should be substituted for the vain traditions received from their fathers. . . .

On the 30th the sun dawned propitiously on the eventful Sabbath. It was one of Fiji's loveliest cloudless days. Early in the morning, the mission families arrived from Viwa, including Mr. and Mrs. Calvert and their children, and Mr. E. P. Martin, whose hearty and praiseworthy labours in the printing department have greatly enriched all Fiji. The word was passed to "beat the drum." The sound thrilled the hearts of all. The two great wooden drums of Fiji, known to the natives by the name of "The Publisher of war," had never before been used but to congregate warriors and cannibals. . . .

The place set apart for the public service was the large dwelling (one hundred and twenty feet by thirty feet) known as the Strangers' House. In front is the Bau assembly-ground, in which the reviews are generally held. At the back are a number of ovens for cooking human flesh, now filled up, it is hoped, for ever. Near these is a large tree, on which are notched the number of those who have been cooked and eaten: it is covered from top to botton with these mementoes of Fijian disgrace. Close by are the evergreen shrubs where certain portions of the eaten parties were hung as ornaments, and were now removed for the first time. This was the spot where the message of love to God and to man was now publicly proclaimed. . . .

The following Sabbath three hundred more embraced Christianity. Next day the temples were spoiled of their ornaments. Prayer was invariably offered to God in each temple before the act was done. Many of the new converts trembled whilst performing the deed. One of the deities, Lauga, the god of rain and of fine weather, was carried in triumph to the mission-house. . . .

[However] whole districts soon joined the enemy, and Bau itself, for the first time since the bloody revolution of 1837, was placed in a state of defence. In the meantime the king gave way to despondency. Only two men in the city openly showed themselves to be friendly to him; the missionary and a faithful Tongan. Yagodamu's house was crowded; and a long array of orphans, whose fathers had been killed by Thakombau, followed his train wherever he went. The king himself and the missionary both thought the hour of vengeance had arrived. I endeavoured to lead the man of blood to repent of his past misdeeds. He spent his days privately with me, no longer concealing his compunction of conscience. It was at length necessary to urge him to attend to the affairs of the state. A friend suggested to Thakombau that Yagodamu would be better employed in reducing the Koro rebels to subjection than in causing fear in Bau by his presence. The cousin [Yagodamu] was therefore despatched on his warlike errand.

Yagodamu did his work leisurely, but well. The rebels had obtained possession of one half of the island at the time of his arrival. But he said that was no matter, they must pray the more; to encourage them, he could tell them that he had heard the missionary say in a sermon that "with God all things are possible." He frightened the enemy as much with his prayers, which he caused to be said before every attack, as by his cannon. He collected heathen troops from Gau and Nairai, and told them to "fight as well as the Christians." In short, he restored confidence to the royal party. The rebels were at last driven into a town, well fortified with a stone wall and cannon. Yagodamu surrounded the fortress, but acted more like Joshua at Jericho than like a Bau chief. Prayer, prayer, prayer, all day along. The heathen portion of his army began to admire the devotion and the apparent faith of the new religionists. Suddenly, when the besieged thought there would be more prayer than battle, the chief ordered an immediate assault, and the place was taken by surprise. All the rebels were spared, although some of the besiegers were clamorous for their extermination. Several hundreds on both sides renounced heathenism, as the sequel of this expedition; and peace was established at Koro.

9 / THE ATTEMPT TO IMPOSE WESTERN STANDARDS

The Western missionaries usually carried a more or less unconscious expectation that any church they would inaugurate would follow in broad outline the church forms they had known in the West. Yet many details of Christian life had to be governed by local circumstances. Missionaries seldom had the power or inclination to attempt the creation of a complete replica of the Western models. Only occasionally was such an ambitious goal undertaken. The principal area in which it was tried during the nineteenth century was in the islands of Polynesia. For a number of reasons these islands were superficially very receptive to alien impositions and the great majority of the people were Christians. Hence it seemed possible here, as nowhere else, for the missionaries to re-create many of the details of Western Christianity. Not only church forms but the full dress and codes of behavior of Christians were adopted from the West.

A description of one of the Christian kingdoms of those islands was written in 1863 by Rufus Anderson, the secretary of the American Board of Commissioners for Foreign Missions in Boston and the most influential American missionary executive of that time. At the age of sixty-six Anderson made a four-month visit to Hawaii in order to decide whether the time had come to put an end to missionary work in those islands and to establish the Hawaiian Church as an autonomous body. He reached the conclusion that such progress had been made by the Church that both these things should be done. He described the religious, social, and political situation which justified such a conclusion, revealing thereby how far the standards of New England had been implanted in the Pacific.

The Hawaiian Theocracy

Could the Hawaiians of 1820 be placed side by side with the present inhabitants of the Islands, the contrast in their outward appearance would be very striking. The dress of the natives of that period was very simple,

From Rufus Anderson, *The Hawaiian Islands: Their Progress and Condition* (Boston: Gould and Lincoln, 1865), pp. 93-94, 95-97, 230, 232, 237-41.

consisting of a *malo* for the male, and a *pa'ū* for the female. The *kihei* was sometimes put on, but not generally; and the children of both sexes were entirely naked till they were nine or ten years old. In bathing in the sea, or sporting in the surf, no articles of clothing were ever worn; and the females were accustomed to leave their pa'ū at their residences, and pass on through the village to the shore, and return in the same manner; and if they were individuals of high rank, they would not unfrequently call at the residence of the missionary to pay their respects, and send a servant to bring the pa'ū, and put it on in the missionary's presence, and return comparatively clad. Such are a few of the outlines of the appearance of the people in regard to their dress.

But what is the appearance of the people now? You will not often see a female without one or two garments of foreign manufacture, and most of the people throughout the Islands are decently clothed. In truth many of them go far beyond their means in this respect. Most of the congregations on the Sabbath exhibit an appearance quite civilized; and one would discover no very wide difference between them and an American assembly. You will seldom see a man or a woman in their ancient costume. This universal custom of wearing clothing, so far as they can obtain it, should be regarded as some proof of advancement. The change from nakedness to the use of decent apparel is certainly very important. . . .

There is scarcely a feature of the generation of 1820 discernible in the one now upon the stage. Then there was no law to regulate society. Now all the natural, social, and domestic relations are respected, and the duties of each are in some measure regulated by good and wholesome statutes; and a neglect to perform the duties attached to these various relations is punishable by fine, imprisonment, or other disabilities. Parents and children, husbands and wives, masters and servants, are recognized in the laws of the nation; and for any delinquency in the performance of their duties they are judicially answerable. No breach of trust or promise, no dereliction of duty, passes unnoticed.

Of common schools there are 336, with 16,153 pupils; and there are also five schools of a higher order, containing 234 scholars. The elements of a common-school education have become pretty generally diffused throughout the nation. Rarely can a child over ten years of age be found who cannot read more or less fluently, while thousands can answer, with a good degree of correctness, miscellaneous questions in the other branches. Sixteen years ago, schools for children were almost unknown, and very few were then able to read. The change is great. We cannot contemplate it without admiring the agency by which it has been wrought; and we feel determined, by help from the Lord, to press forward this department of our labor, until the blessing of a good education shall be enjoyed by every child. . . .

On the first arrival of the missionaries, the people were a nation of drunkards; and every vice was practised, and every crime was committed, which grows out of such a state of things. In every village the most disgusting licentiousness might be seen, the legitimate and never-failing accompaniment of intemperance. These abominations were not confined to common people; but the kings and the chiefs were the principal actors in the riotous scenes of those days. The eye saw and the ear heard many things which may not be uttered or written. The tongue would falter to speak them, and the paper itself would blush to receive the record.

Has any change been effected in the habits of the Islanders in this respect? Is every village now, as formerly, filled with intoxicated and licentious revellers? Not at all. There has been a great, nay, a mighty revolution. There has been a transition from brutal intoxication to Christian sobriety. It is a rare occurrence to see a drunken native. The scale is turned. The foreign community are the consumers of intoxicating drinks. There is no nation on the globe that better deserves the appellation of "temperate," than the Hawaiian; and they would be more consistently and entirely so, if they were left to manage the subject for themselves, without foreign interference. But, alas! the Hawaiian government has not the liberty to make any article of commerce contraband. . . .

Their social condition, though far from what it should be, is yet a great improvement on the past. Scarcely forty years have elapsed since the first marriage. Prior to that there was no connection between man and woman that could not be sundered at any moment by the will of the parties; and this led to frequent crimes and great misery. Among the earliest blessings on a large scale, introduced by missionaries, was Christian marriage. Two thousand marriages were solemnized in the single year following June, 1830. The number reported during the last ten years is six thousand seven hundred and nineteen; and the contract has been recognized and confirmed by the laws for more than thirty years, so that it could not be annulled by the parties. . . .

While the instructions to the first missionaries enjoined upon them the grand aim "of raising up the whole people of the Islands to an elevated state of Christian civilization," they were also required to "withhold themselves entirely from all interference and intermeddling with the political affairs and party concerns of the nation." This they have done. But they were not thus shut off from all attempts to enlighten and elevate the government of the Islands, since that was indispensable to the attainment, by the people, of an elevated Christian civilization. The government could not remain unchanged, and the people become free and civilized. The people must own property, have acknowledged rights, and be governed by written, well-known, established laws. This was far from their condition before the year 1838. The government was then a despotism. The will of the king was law, his power absolute; and this was true of the chiefs, also, in their separate spheres, so far as the common people were concerned. All rights of property, in the last resort, was with the king. How were the people to attain the true Christian position? Obviously the rulers had duties to learn and to perform, equally with the people; and the missionaries were the Christian teachers of both classes, with God's Word for their guide. . . .

The following Bill of Rights was signed by the king on the 7th of June, 1839, and was the first essential departure from the ancient despotism:

God has made of one blood all nations of men, to dwell on the face of the earth in unity and blessedness. God has also bestowed certain rights alike on all men, and all chiefs, and all people, of all lands.

These are some of the rights which he has given alike to every man and every chief, namely, life, limb, liberty, the labor of his hands, and the productions of his mind.

God has also established governments and rulers for the purposes of peace; but, in making laws for a nation, it is by no means proper to enact laws for the protection of rulers only, without also providing protection for their subjects; neither is it proper to enact laws to enrich the chiefs only, without regard to the enriching of their subjects also; and hereafter there shall by no means be any law enacted which is inconsistent with what is above expressed; neither shall any tax be assessed, nor any service or labor required of any man, in any manner at variance with the above sentiments.

These sentiments are hereby proclaimed for the purpose of protecting all alike, both the people and the chiefs of all these Islands, that no chief may be able to oppress any subject, but that the chiefs and people may enjoy the same protection under the same law.

Protection is hereby secured to the persons of all the people, together with their lands, their building lots, and all their property; and nothing whatever shall be taken from any individual, except by express provision of the laws.

Whatever chief shall perseveringly act in violation of this constitution, shall no longer remain a chief of the Sandwich Islands; and the same shall be true of the governors, officers, and all land agents.

This *Magna Charta* of the Hawaiian Islands was conferred voluntarily, without the intervention of armed barons and their retainers; and perhaps it might be difficult to find such another instance of the cheerful surrender of arbitrary power, purely out of regard to the welfare and happiness of the subjects.

On the 8th of October, 1840, Kamehameha conferred a constitution on the people, recognizing the three grand divisions of a civilized monarchy —king, legislature, and judges—and defining, in some respects, the duties of each. The constitution of 1840 declared that "no law shall be enacted which is at variance with the Word of the Lord Jehovah, or with the general spirit of his Word," and that "all laws of the islands shall be in consistency with the general spirit of God's law." The laws must of course have been imperfect, because they were framed with reference to the low condition of the people, and what it seemed then possible to carry into effect. They were severe upon the prevalent and destructive vices of intemperance and licentiousness. And was it not something to succeed (as they did) in driving those shameless vices into concealment? One of the first inflictions of the death penalty, for the infraction of these laws, was upon a chief of high rank, a favorite of the king, for murdering his wife by poison. He and his accomplice, after a regular trial and condemnation in a court composed of Kekuanaoa, governor of Oahu, as presiding judge, and a jury of twelve Hawaiians, were hung on the walls of the fort. . . . [A] code of laws was adopted by the "nobles and representatives of the Hawaiian Islands, in legislative council assembled," April 27, 1846. A few of the more important statutes concerning religious matters will be quoted.

1. The religion of the Lord Jesus Christ shall continue to be the established national religion of the Hawaiian Islands. The laws of Kamehameha III., orally proclaimed, abolishing all idol-worship and ancient heathen customs, are hereby continued in force. . . .

2. Although the Protestant religion is the religion of the government, as heretofore proclaimed, nothing in the last preceding section shall be construed as requiring any particular form of worship, neither is anything therein contained to be construed as connecting the ecclesiastical with the body politic. All men residing in this kingdom shall be allowed freely to worship the God of the Christian Bible according to the dictates of their own consciences. . . .

3. It shall not be lawful to violate the Christian Sabbath by the transaction of worldly business. The Sabbath shall be considered no day in law. All documents and other evidences of worldly transactions dated on the Sabbath shall be deemed in law to have no date, and to be void for not having legal existence. . . .

10 / THE NATURE OF "MASS MOVEMENTS" IN ASIA

The missionaries who came from the West into Asia and Africa were nurtured in a highly individualistic form of Christianity. The Evangelical Revival, which lay back of the missionary movement, stressed the experience of individual conversion and individual growth in the Christian life. Western culture as a whole was at that time in its most individualistic stage. Yet the missionaries entered into societies which had a far more collective approach to life. Religion was a matter of group experience, and religious decisions, like most decisions of importance, were taken by the group. Western Christians were not always ready to appreciate this style of life and method of decision.

Yet, when there came large accessions to Christianity, they usually grew out of what were basically group decisions. Though they seldom involved a ruler and his whole country, they often involved large sections of a tribe or ethnic group. In Burma it was the Karen people among whom the movement toward Christianity first took root, and later developments of Burmese Christianity took place among other tribal peoples who had a strong group consciousness. Similarly, in Sumatra it was among a part of the Batak people, the Toba Bataks, that the largest of the new churches of Asia originated. In India, where society had been traditionally divided into castes, it was natural that decisions with regard to Christianity be made by caste groups.

The Western missionaries in India in the nineteenth century did not at first think in terms of conversion by caste groups. They addressed their message to individuals. They fought the appearance of caste distinctions in the Church, and through their educational and social work they tried to minimize the influence of caste in society at large. But sometimes this very opposition to caste consciousness gave Christianity a strong appeal to those lower caste groups who found themselves victimized by the caste system. They turned to Christianity as a way of liberation. So, starting principally in the 1870s and increasing through the first quarter of the twentieth century, there came a movement of low caste or outcaste people into the Church. These groups, like the Karens and tribal folk of

Burma, had the least to lose in the existing structures of society and hence were most ready to respond to the possibility of change.

At first the missionaries were reluctant to accept these "mass movements." In addition to their hesitations regarding group conversions, they feared that if Christianity were represented overwhelmingly by the poorest and most ignorant elements, it would have no influence in society and would be automatically rejected by more affluent and cultured people. As time passed, however, a greater interest developed in the challenge and opportunity for service among the poorer groups, and missionaries were assigned to mass movement work. Among these were women such as the author of the following passage. She was an Englishwoman who chose to live under the most primitive village conditions in order to serve the Chamars, or leather workers, and also the even more depressed sweepers. These two castes belonged to what has been traditionally the outcaste segment of society. She presents here the story of an incipient but ultimately unsuccessful mass movement among them. The dilemmas she describes are revealing not only of the dilemmas of Christians in collectivist societies but of those of all Christians faced with the moral ambiguities of social life.

A Woman Missionary's Description

In at least five . . . villages groups of Chamars were strongly urging the community to take the decisive step of baptism. Others felt they must consider very carefully before committing themselves in any way. Many methods of petty persecution were open to the farmer when his serfs tried to break away. Many Chamars had taken the step at one time or another, and had found it impossible to stand out against the persecution that followed. In Jaipur itself, a number had become Christians a dozen years ago, but had all come back. In Sherola, twenty-five years ago, about a score of them became Christians, but only two or three managed to stick to it. If all the Chamars in all the villages round would agree to become Christians, then it would be easy. Better wait a while and see what the others were going to do. The Christian preacher himself seemed to think this the wisest plan.

As we sat in the courtyard of his house one day we asked him about the village councils from which he had expected such great things a short while back. "I'm watching and waiting," he answered. "They had an Arya Samāj [reformed Hindu] man along to their council the other day, and now some of them are more inclined to become Aryas than

From Miriam Young, *Seen and Heard in a Punjab Village* (London: SCM Press Ltd., 1931), pp. 137-44, 146-48, 151-54. Reprinted by permission of the publisher.

Christians. The others wanted me to baptize them at once, and said they ought not to be made to wait for the waverers. But I said to them, 'When you are all ready for baptism, I will baptize you, and not till then. If some of you become Christians and some do not, these others will become your enemies and make difficulties and you will get drawn back again.' This appeared to be quite sound strategy, but was it, we wondered, sound Christianity? The problem came still nearer home to us. Quite early one morning a Chamar came to our door. A poor type of man was the impression given by a casual observation of him. He was not one we had had much to do with, for he was not one of those learning to read, and he did not seem to be held of much account amongst the others. Quite abruptly he presented his request. "Make us Christians, Miss Sa'b. Make us all Christians." "You don't understand what you're talking about," I rejoined. "Yes, I do. We all want to be Christians, all of us. We're not going to do forced labour for the farmers any more with their two penny wage. We'll become Christians. We've talked it over and decided."

"That shows you don't understand," I answered, and went on to explain to him why it was not in our power to make a Christian of anybody, that it was a matter of one's heart going out to Jesus Christ and His teaching, and of one's own desire and resolve to follow in His way.

"Yes," he said, "that's what we're going to do. We're going to follow in His way."

"But you don't even know what His way is?" I objected. "If you want to learn, of course we'll teach you. It's just what we're longing for, to find people who want to learn His way. We're ready enough to teach you and give you all the help we can. That's what we're here for. If you're really in earnest, you can come to us, or we'll come to you, and teach you as much and as often as you like. As for following in His way, you can begin at once. It isn't a matter of baptism and of coming out of one brotherhood into another, you can be a Christian in your own brotherhood, just where you are." . . .

We hardly knew whether to attach much importance to this incident or not. We had been working and hoping for this very thing, not only among the Chamars, but in Khera generally, working to quicken a spirit of inquiry which should lead people to seek for further teaching. We had dreamed many dreams of how this might come about. Was this perhaps the beginning of some of our dreams coming true? On the other hand, the obvious motive which lay behind the request did not look much like a genuine spirit of inquiry. For some time we had been giving series of readings from the Gospel in different quarters of the village. So we decided to respond to their request, and in a measure test the sincerity of it, by offering to give the next series in their quarter. This offer was welcomed, and a fortnight later we started. Every day at midday we sat outside their principal workshop and read a portion of Mark's Gospel, adapting the language a little, and sometimes adding a few words of explanation. We also sang a few hymns. The men would bring their shoes outside and sit and work as we read. A few women would stand for a bit and listen, and nearly all the children in the place used to come and play about in the dust at our feet. Several times one man would turn to another and say:

"Yes. We'll become Christians. Yes, this is the way we'll follow," and we always said, "Yes do! Why not? It's the way of truth and salvation."

When we had nearly finished our readings they made a more definite request, saying that they had talked it over, and were all agreed that they wanted to be made Christians. Yes, they knew it was a matter of the heart, of living according to His teaching. They were prepared to do that. We could keep on coming as we had been doing for the last fortnight and teach them His way. They wanted to be made one of us. Such a definite request embarrassed us. We could not reject it. We did not know how to respond to it. They welcomed a suggestion we made of a Sunday service, and the next Sunday we started it. We had a good deal of singing, for many of the hymns had now become familiar and were very popular. Somebody found a drum, and there were two dilapidated-looking instruments hanging on the walls of the workshop, a kind of fiddle with only two strings, which Kalli, with his usual versatility, was learning to play. So the musical part of the service went with a great swing. . . .

"If we do become Christians what benefit will it be to us!" asked Nannhua thoughtfully after the first Sunday service. Was he merely weighing advantage with disadvantage, or was he counting the cost? I believe they were sincere in their request as far as they understood. But they understood very little. They were prepared to honour their obligations, but their ideas of what those obligations might be were often extraordinarily astray. We felt that their attitude was at least hopeful in this respect, that it gave us the opportunity of sowing seed, some of which we hoped might chance to fall in fruitful ground. But our opportunity seemed suddenly and almost inexplicably to vanish.

It was some few weeks later that one of the Marwar missionaries and the preacher from Jaipur, in the course of a tour which had as one of its objects the exploration of the situation with regard to the Chamars, came to Khera. They went into the Chamar quarter to preach, and to sound their hearers on their attitude towards Christianity. In response to an appeal from the missionary to come out of their old community and become Christians they announced with great decision and energy. "We're not going to become Christians."

"There is no other village in the district," said the missionary to us, almost reproachfully, "where we have met with a response of that kind." We were of course puzzled as to what it meant. We remembered that previous to this at Christmas time the same response had been made by one of our night school boys to a similar appeal. But it appears to me now, as I consider the order of events, that the reason for this apparent inconsistency and change of attitude may have been the baptism of the Jaipur sweepers which took place shortly before Christmas. Our boys had questioned us very closely about it, and I imagine it came as rather a blow to them to realize that in throwing in their lot with Christians they might have to throw in their lot with sweepers. We had made occasional efforts to persuade them to let us invite the sweepers to the Sunday service, and had tried to make them realize that the way they said they wanted to follow was the way of brotherhood to all men, and must include the sweepers. But they had quite declined to have anything to do with sweepers, and understanding how hard it must be for them to give up their one claim to superiority we were prepared to wait. But we felt that here lay the acid test of their Christianity. . . .

Some fortnight later nearly all the Chamars from Rahimpur, a village ten miles away from us, and the other side of Jaipur, were baptized. They, like the Chamars in so many villages, had been discussing the matter for several months. Unlike the other villages they had been able to achieve unity amongst themselves, and just before Christmas they had signed their name or put their thumb print to a petition addressed to the Marwar church begging for baptism and fellowship in the Church.

I sat through the Church meeting at which their request was considered. My mind was full of doubts and questionings. These poor downtrodden outcaste people! How legitimate and worthy that they should respond to the preaching of the Fatherhood of God and the brotherhood of men, and see there the means to escape from their degradation and to rise in the social scale. Their poverty and ignorance were the direct result of their having been thrust outside the pale of society. How natural they should seek by any means open to them to come within it! That all kinds of hopes and desires were mixed up in this decision to become

Christians seemed to me beyond dispute; that spiritual motives were present alongside many others I was convinced. But had their essential attitude really anything more to do with becoming disciples of Jesus Christ in His own sense than had the attitude of the crowds of His own day, who hung upon Him listening and pressed upon Him to touch Him and desired to take Him by force to make Him a King? Was there perhaps in this apparent day of opportunity a temptation akin to that of which Jesus Christ seemed to be constantly aware, and which He resisted so unswervingly? Yet how impossible for us as Christians to see these Chamars, bitten by a great desire for escape and betterment, making all kinds of efforts to find some means of emancipation, appealing to us for help, and yet to sit still and do nothing particular. It seemed to me that the Church was saying, "If only they will become Christians we shall be able to give them all the help they want." I felt it was essential that we should make it clear that the gifts of friendship and brotherhood and social betterment which they sought, and which were in our hands to give, we gave freely, because *we* were Christians, not because we hoped *they* were, or were going to be.

There was a consensus of opinion in our church that people wishing to be baptized must be adequately taught. Who could quarrel with such an opinion? It was decided that this petition from the Chamars was to be met by an offer of concentrated teaching for a month. Members of the church were to visit them as frequently as possible and teach them. Certain mission workers were to be set free from other work to concentrate on this. . . .

Six weeks later they were baptized, seventy-four of them, men and women. Many of the women had taken fright at the last moment and had run away and hidden in their houses. After several of the men had been baptized, the preacher, noting the women's absence, and feeling that without the women's co-operation the whole movement would fall to the ground, asked some of his helpers to go and bring the women back. It is easy to understand the shrinking these women felt, the publicity of the ceremony made it foreign to their ways of doing things, and at times of stage fright it does sometimes seem as though a shove and a push may be what is needed rather than argument and persuasion. But it was disquieting to hear in Khera the report that the women had been baptized by force; that they had refused and run away, but the Miss Sahib and the Bible woman had gone and dragged them out of their houses, and compelled them. We knew the missionary better than that; still that was the impression that had been received by onlookers.

After this decisive step by the Chamars of Rahimpur, the other villagers seemed to agree to sit down and await developments. "See how the Rahimpur folk get on, then we can make up our own minds." It is just possible that the knowledge that Rahimpur was prepared to act as a kind of test case may have partly influenced our Khera folk in their decision not to commit themselves in any way at present.

My knowledge of what happened afterwards in Rahimpur is all second-hand. Almost immediately a storm of persecution arose. The Jāts [farmers] said, "You'll do no more forced labour for us? Very well, then you shall no longer have any rights or privileges in this village." They were not allowed to graze their cattle on common land, not allowed to bring in fuel from the fields or the jungle. If they got out of their own quarters into neighbouring fields or jungle it was by stealth. Access to wells which they had regarded as their own was denied them, debts of long standing were suddenly foreclosed, land which they were renting was seized from them, individuals were beaten and their property looted. One missionary very pluckily went to live with them, putting up with most cramped quarters in the midst of their houses, and though the Jāts at first remained friendly to her, and wished to give her freedom to go how and where she pleased, she declined to have any special privileges, declaring that she was now a Chamar among Chamars. She shared to the utmost in her power the calamities their baptism had brought upon them. Here at least was something of permanent gain, nothing that came afterwards could undo that. Any kind of brotherliness and friendliness other Christians could show to these people in such difficult circumstances would naturally be worth a great deal. It is not perhaps surprising, though in my judgment it was a disastrous mistake, that some of those who represented both the church and mission felt it necessary to intercede for them with the Government official against the farmers, and that the preacher should encourage some of them to take the disputes over land into court, and promise them all possible support. It turned the Jāts' attitude into one of bitterness against the missionaries and other Christian workers, and made it impossible to see in the Chamars' firmness under this persecution an undoubted proof of their loyalty to Christ.

It sometimes seemed to us that this persecution had very little directly to do with their Christianity. It was their attitude to their masters in general, and to "forced labour" in particular, that roused the antagonism of the Jāts. What did it matter to a Jāt what a Chamar chose to do or believe, or by what name he chose to call himself, so long as he remained an obedient serf? If the church could have persuaded the Chamars to accept their position for Christ's sake, and to adopt towards their serfdom the attitude which St. Paul tried to induce in those Christians who had been called "being bond-servants," they would, it seemed to us, have had no special persecution to bear. Of persecution from their own community we heard nothing.

I do not know by what gradual steps the situation altered and the Chamars began to go back upon their profession of faith. For some time we kept on hearing reports that they had all gone back and had become Arya Samājists. These reports were often denied. But by the end of five months it was acknowledged on every hand that the Aryas had held a special Shuddhi ceremony, and had received into fellowship all those who had retracted their profession of Christianity. This included practically the whole community. There were some who declared that they had been unwilling to retract, but that the headmen had included their names in the list, and they had been forced into it against their will. There were others who excused themselves on the ground that they were Christians still at heart, but that the Jāts made it impossible for them to live so long as they made outward profession of the fact. Let them get the next harvest safely gathered in, and they would once more boldly take their stand as Christians no matter what anyone might say.

VARIATIONS AND MODIFICATIONS OF CHRISTIANITY

11 / A CHINESE DEVIATION

The nineteenth and early twentieth centuries, as has already been suggested, were not outstanding for experimentation and modification in Christianity as it encountered non-Western cultures. However, on the fringes of Church and mission, or in societies where Western influence was still weak, some significant variations nonetheless appeared.

The most important of the movements which arose on the fringes of Christianity was that of the Taiping, or Great Peace, in China in the middle decades of the nineteenth century. It was led by Hung Hsui-ch'üan (or Hung-sieu-tsiuen as the name appears in the following account), an enigmatic and visionary character who had received Christian instruction from Issacher Roberts, a Baptist missionary in Canton. On the basis of his visions he organized a messianic religious body holding beliefs very close to those of Christians and claiming to possess the true form of Christianity. The members regarded themselves as destined by God to establish their rule over the world. Their armies were amazingly success-

ful, and for a period of years they controlled central and southern China with their capital established at Nanking. Eventually the imperial troops, with some Western aid, crushed them.

Mr. Roberts spent some time at the Taiping capital, on the invitation of Hung, with the hope of bringing the movement to purer Christian beliefs. A few other missionaries also visited Nanking. One of these was Joseph Edkins of the London Missionary Society, who came in the spring of 1861. The following extract is taken from Edkins' report. From it much can be discerned of the beliefs and practices of this peculiar form of Chinese Christianity.

Visit to the Taiping

Our long journey in chairs was at last nearly completed, by our arrival at the south-east corner of the city. We had left the Ming tombs, and the hills in which they were embosomed, behind on our right, and proceeded along the south wall, outside the broad moat which skirts it. Three-quarters of a mile conducted us to the vicinity of the principal gate on the south side. A long street leading to it was crowded with traffickers. Fresh provisions were heaped on either side of the road. The shops were stocked with clothing and shoes. Red and yellow silk and calico were piled on shelves, ready for the extensive and indiscriminate use of these articles by the Taipings. The bearers pushed their way through the crowd of rebel soldiers and villagers, too busily engaged in buying and selling to give much heed to the foreign visitors suddenly coming among them. A multitude of ponies, ridden by men and women in rebel costume, were swiftly crossing in various directions the open spaces at the bridge, and in front of the gate. We threaded our way carefully between them, and passed through the long and imposing city entrance without challenge from the janiters and watch-beaters, that had often checked us on our way. . . .

A broad paved street . . . conducted us without turning for a mile. Then we proceeded to the left, and after another mile reached the Kan-wang's palace. Here we expected to find the relatives of that chief, and also Mr. Roberts the missionary, whose relations with Hung-sieu-tsiuen have become so widely known. That the Kan-wang, "Shield Prince," was absent, we felt to be a misfortune. An old acquaintance of my own at Shanghai, a baptized convert at Hongkong, in good standing

From Joseph Edkins, "Narrative of a Visit to Nanking." *In Chinese Scenes and People* by Jane R. Edkins (London: James Nisbet and Co., 1863), pp. 263-65, 269-70, 272-79.

for several years in the community of native Christians there gathered, a catechist of the London Missionary Society there, and as such trusted and respected in a high degree, his presence would have been welcome. The necessities of the Taiping warfare, and the politics of Nanking, had obliged him to leave recently for an army in the south.

Opposite the *fu*, which is occupied as a residence by the Kan-wang, was a painted wall, decorated with fantastic figures, and having an immense character in the centre, known as *fuh*, and signifying happiness. The eight beatitudes of the fifth chapter of Matthew were also written on tablets in gilt letters—a public indication of the anxiety felt by Hung-jen, the "Shield King," to maintain the authority of Christ as the great teacher of mankind. . . .

The evening was spent in reading over letters to Hung-sieu-tsiuen from Mr. Roberts, and the answers. Among other matters, the attention of the chief had been called to the titles he had bestowed on the eastern king. This deceased champion of the Taipings is styled by the chief, "Saviour from disease." This was shown by Mr. Roberts to be improper, as placing him in comparison of Christ, who will not give his glory to another, and who is the only Saviour. To this the vermilion reply is, that the eastern king was the beloved Son of God, and that, though he does not save from sin, he saves from sickness.

Another subject taken up was the Church and its Head. It consists of converted men, of such as are regenerated by the Holy Spirit, and baptized. Christ alone is the Head of the Church. To this it is replied, that the church referred to by the American teacher of the holy doctrine is the spiritual Church, while that which he (the chief) is seeking to establish in the world is the temporal universal church or kingdom, of which the Heavenly Father, the Heavenly Brother (Jesus), himself and his son, a sacred quaternion, are the common head.

His mode of writing is thoroughly respectful and friendly in its tone. He looks upon the Christians of England and America as those who have had Christianity in its earlier forms, and as good men who seek the welfare of the Chinese by teaching them the true religion. But he looks on himself as divinely appointed, in subordination only to Christ himself, to destroy idolatry, and to be the head of a regenerated world. He has divine authority (so in his madness he is convinced) to impose on the world new revelations, and found "the heavenly kingdom of great peace" (Taiping-tien-kwo). He cannot, therefore, in replying to the communications of missionaries, do other than repeat these pretensions, based on his visions, and add, as he best can, arguments in self-defence, derived from his careful and extended reading of the Holy Scriptures. . . .

The evening of the [next] day was occupied in part with the perusal of edicts from the insurgent chief to Mr. Roberts. One contained nine reasons for maintaining that Christ is inferior to the Father. In another he said, "The Heavenly Father is my own father, and Christ my own brother, born of the same mother. I am made ruler by the Father and Brother, to testify to the gospel, and destroy the works of the devil." Elsewhere he says, in defence of his visions, "In the Revelation of John, John saw with his own eyes the Lamb standing before the Father. The Lamb is the Elder Brother." He also says, "I have written to you many letters. Do you cordially recognise the fact that I have gone to heaven, or do you not? Do you, with all the western brethren, perceive my meaning? Do you acknowledge the holy will of God? Think of the risen sun (the chief himself) shining in the heavens. Will you not awake? Will you not believe? Believe for happiness. Add faithfulness to faithfulness, and loyalty to loyalty. Then you shall see greater things than these."

It was in this tone that the missionary was addressed, from the depths of the Nanking imperial residence, by his quondam pupil. The disciple has become a divinely-commissioned prophet, who has gone up to heaven, at the time of a trance, and there seen God, and been informed that he was himself a son of God, and brother of Jesus.

Such was the effect of Christian teaching on the mind of a visionary, who, by the report of what he saw when in a distempered state of mind and body, attached to him a band of deluded and devoted followers. First he met with Christian books. Then came visions. Then followed his intercourse with the missionary at Canton, who did not comprehend much of his extraordinary story. After this ensued another period of seclusion at his native village near Canton. He receives revelations, becomes a sect-founder, communicates his enthusiasm to his adherents, and then emerges from his obscurity to undertake the achievement, by force of arms, of a political and religious revolution in the country. . . .

While Mr. Roberts remained in Nanking (for he has now returned to Canton), it was in this tone that he was addressed by the chief, who regarded him with great partiality, on account of a revelation made to him, "that Mr. Roberts was a good man." On one occasion, in consequence of this favour, he was admitted to a personal interview. The difficulty in arranging the interview, was in the persistent refusal of the missionary to kneel to the Taiping chief. After consultation between the high chiefs, or kings, it was agreed that he need not kneel. He was told, however, that all present would kneel to the Heavenly Father, and that he could not decline to do so likewise. Even this, however, he would not undertake to do, for fear of being misunderstood. On entering the hall of audience, he stood at the end of one of the long rows of high officials, who were ranged to the number of about twenty, on the east and west sides of the hall. All, including the missionary, appeared in their court-robes. When the time of worship came, Kan-wang, the *ci-devant* preacher in the London Mission at Hongkong, called out in a loud voice from where he stood, near the principal chief, "Lo-hiau-tsiuen pai Tien fu"—*Mr. Roberts, worship the Heavenly Father*. Taken by surprise, the missionary, after a moment's hesitation, knelt, with his face turned away from Hung-sieu-tsiuen, while Kan-wang offered an extemporaneous prayer. Then all rose, and made many genuflexions to Hung-sieu-tsiuen, the missionary alone excepted. A long conversation ensued between these old acquaintances. The Tien-wang asked if Mr. Roberts remembered him, who replied that he scarcely did. Many years had elapsed, and there was a great difference in their appearance.

There were strange anomalies in this audience hall. Perhaps the strangest of them all was, that these chiefs should make an extemporaneous prayer to Almighty God, by one of their number, a part of their court ceremony, when paying a state visit to their lord paramount. The prayer, too, would be no medley of blasphemous expressions, such as many would expect from men like the Taipings, but would consist of appropriate Christian sentiments, such as the converts of the Protestant missionaries learn to use. Such is the prayer the same chief has published in a recent book, and such was the prayer which I myself heard offered by him as a part of his daily worship months before in the city of Sucheu.

The next morning was Saturday (March 23), the rebel Sabbath. We heard that the young chief before mentioned, the son of one of the so-called "kings," was to preach on the parade ground. Proceeding there we found a large concourse of Taipings. A sea of flags and streamers, red, yellow, white, and green, floated in the wind over them. There was also an assemblage of horses and sedan-chairs. The preacher of the day, who is also in temporary charge of the affairs of the city, and whom we had visited on our arrival, came in a large yellow chair. Beneath the open sky there was a platform made of square tables, and a table on these covered with a red and yellow cloth. On this the preacher stood with his pasteboard yellow coronet, and addressed the listening crowd for twenty minutes. He spoke on the soldier's daily duties, his care of his family, attention to prayer in the night at the appointed time and observance of the watchword when on guard.

The orator spoke with a week voice and hesitating manner. He was followed by a more fluent speaker, a high chief, middle-aged, who discussed various moral and political matters. He gave reasons for the exclusion of traders from the city, except such as dealt in medicines, and mentioned locations in which trade may be carried on without the walls. He also referred to the practice of women riding to market; the elder women might do so, but it was not becoming for such as were still young. They had better not be seen in public. He also urged the cultivation of a kind spirit towards the aged and destitute, of whom there were many, and he urged that their case demanded sympathy and aid.

After these addresses, all the listeners, standing on the green sward of the review ground, within a large semicircle of flaunting banners, knelt towards the table where the young chief also knelt. There was silence for a few minutes, as if they were all praying to the Heavenly Father. Then they rose and separated, feeling perhaps that when a political and moral exhortation had been delivered, and a silent prayer offered to the Heavenly Father, the object of the assembly was gained. . . .

Sunday, March 24. Large audiences gathered round us in the streets while we stood at convenient points and preached Jesus and eternal life. That the most of the Taipings are very ignorant of Christianity, may be gathered from their answers to inquiries. A soldier, when asked, Who is the Holy Spirit? replied, "The Eastern King." Such ignorance is the result of the unhappy errors of the insurgent chief, who has misunderstood the doctrine of the Trinity, failed to apprehend the distinction of the Persons, and interpreted the promise of our Saviour respecting the Comforter as having its fulfilment in the person of one of his own first followers.

A religious service was held at our lodging and another in a large building, part of which was called the "Hall of the Heavenly Father," and part the "Hall of Worship." Many were present to hear.

In the afternoon, in conversation with the young chief who had preached the day before, I remarked, that a proclamation recently issued by him contained much which appeared to us to be very excellent, recommending, as it did, kindness to the poor and unfortunate. He said, in reply, that it was according to the nature of the Christian religion to be benevolent, and that Jesus came into the world to save and bless men; for this he had died on the cross.

In answer, I said that I was delighted to hear him speak in this manner. It was what we felt to be most important truth; and I would beg to ask, why, having such views, he did not refer yesterday, while preaching to the soldiers, to the crucifixion and atonement of Jesus; for I had noticed that he spoke only of moral and political duties. He said that the officers were all expected to teach these doctrines, each in his own house, on occasions when the family met for daily worship and instruction. They did so to a great extent. He then expressed his satisfaction that foreign teachers came to teach what is good, and to do good, thus doing what was very meritorious. . . .

During the next two days some of the notable spots in this vast and ancient city were visited. Where the porcelain tower once stood, there is now a mass of glazed bricks, whole and broken, white and coloured. The Taiping people, had they the power, would destroy all the idol temples and pagodas in China. Their religious fanaticism is too essential a part of the movement to allow of any change in this point. If they are to be exterminated by their opponents, they will continue to be iconoclasts, as they will continue to call themselves Christians till their power is broken.

12 / AN INDIAN REINTERPRETATION

India, too, produced distinctive ways of appropriating and adapting Christianity. From Ram Mohun Roy at the beginning of the nineteenth century to Mahatma Gandhi in the twentieth, the leaders of Indian religious and political thought lived in dialogue with Christianity. Some of them claimed to have a truer view of Christianity than that which was to be found in the westernized churches of Asia.

The movement which came closest to Christianity was the Brahmo Samaj founded by Ram Mohun Roy. It had its chief strength among the Bengali intellectuals who stood at the center of the currents of Indian thought in the nineteenth century. It represented the beginning of a creative Indian response to the West and hence played a significant part in the formation of modern India. In a characteristically Hindu way, it accepted Jesus as a revelation of God alongside of other revelations in other traditions. It was vigorously monotheistic and laid much stress on

*ethics. One of its most famous leaders was Keshub Chunder Sen, who
lectured widely both in India and in England and eventually founded a
separate branch of the society. The following selection from one of Sen's
lectures entitled "Jesus Christ: Europe and Asia," delivered in Calcutta
in 1866, reveals something of how such men viewed Jesus and what they
regarded as important in His life.*

Keshub Chunder Sen on Jesus Christ

I shall not enter into the details of his life and ministry, as my present
business is simply with the influence which he exercised on the world. It
cannot be denied that it was solely for his thorough devotion to the
cause of truth, and the interests of suffering humanity, that he patiently
endured all the privations and hardships which came in his way, and
met that fierce storm of persecution which his infuriated antagonists
poured on his devoted head. (Hear, hear.) It was from no selfish impulse,
from no spirit of mistaken fanaticism, that he bravely and cheerfully
offered himself to be crucified on the cross. He laid down his life that
God might be glorified. (Hear, hear.) I have always regarded the cross
as a beautiful emblem of self-sacrifice unto the glory of God—one which
is calculated to quicken the higher feelings and aspirations of the heart,
and to purify the soul; and I believe there is not a heart, how callous
and hard soever it may be, that can look with cold indifference on that
grand and significant symbol. (Applause.) Such honourable and disinterested self-sacrifice has produced, as might be anticipated, wonderful
results; the noble purpose of Christ's noble heart has been fully achieved,
as the world's history will testify. The vast moral influence of his life
and death still lives in human society, and animates its movements. It
has moulded the civilization of modern Europe, and it underlies the
many civilizing and philanthropic agencies of the present day. He has
exercised such living and lasting influence on the world, not by the
physical miracles which popular theology has ascribed to him, but by the
greater miracle of the truth which he preached. If faith cannot remove
mountains, I do not know what can. There is indeed a power in truth,
far above the might of princes and potentates, which can work wonders
and achieve impossibilities; and it was surely with this power that Jesus
triumphantly established the kingdom of God. (Cheers.) He was the son
of an humble carpenter, and he laboured in connection with his ministry
only for three short years—do not these simple facts conclusively prove,

From Keshub Chunder Sen, *The Brahmo Samaj. Lectures and Tracts. First and
Second Series,* edited by Sophia Dobson Collet (London: Strahan and Co., Publishers,
1870), pp. 8-10, 31-35.

when viewed in reference to the vast amount of influence he has exercised on the world, that greatness dwelt in Jesus? (Applause.) Poor and illiterate, brought up in Nazareth—a village notorious for corruption —under demoralizing influences, his associates the lowest mechanics and fishermen, from whom he could receive not a single ray of enlightenment, he rose superior to all outward circumstances by the force of his innate greatness, and grew in wisdom, faith, and piety by meditation and prayer, and with the inspiration of the Divine spirit working within him. Though all the external conditions of his life were against him, he rose above them with the strength of the Lord, and, with almost superhuman wisdom and energy, taught those sublime truths and performed those moral wonders for which succeeding generations have paid him the tribute of admiration and gratitude. (Cheers.) Verily he was above ordinary humanity. Sent by Providence to reform and regenerate mankind, he received from Providence wisdom and power for that great work; and throughout his career and ministration, and in the subsequent effects of his grand movement, we find positive evidence of that miraculous power with which inspired greatness vanquishes mighty potentates, hurls down dynasties, and uproots kingdoms, and builds up, from chaos and corruption the kingdom of truth and God, of freedom and harmony. (Cheers.) . . .

I cherish great respect for the Europeans, not for any secular considerations, but for the sake of Jesus Christ, whom they profess to follow, and whom, I believe, it is their mission to make known to us in words as well as deeds. It is the bounden duty of all Europeans in India so to prove their fidelity to him in all the avocations of their private and public life, that through the influence of their example the spirit of true Christian righteousness may leaven native society. I regard every European settler in India as a missionary of Christ, and I have a right to demand that he should always remember and act up to his high responsibilities. (Applause.) But, alas! owing to the reckless conduct of a number of pseudo-Christians, Christianity has failed to produce any wholesome moral influence on my countrymen. (Hear, hear—"They are nominal Christians.") Yea, their muscular Christianity has led many a native to identify the religion of Jesus with the power and privilege of inflicting blows and kicks with impunity! (Deafening cheers.) And thus Jesus has been dishonoured in India, and thus, alas! the true spirit of his religion has been lost upon the natives through the recklessness of a host of nominal Christians. Behold Christ's Church in danger! Behold Christ crucified in the lives of those who profess to be his followers!

Had it not been for them, the name of Jesus Christ would have been ten times more glorified than it seems to have been. (Hear, hear.) I hope that, for India's sake, for Christ's sake, for truth's sake. The Christians in India should conscientiously strive to realize in their lives the high morality of the Gospel. . . . If, however, our Christian friends persist in traducing our nationality and national character, and in distrusting and hating Orientalism, let me assure them that I do not in the least feel dishonoured by such imputations. On the contrary, I rejoice, yea, I am proud, that I am an Asiatic. And was not Jesus Christ an Asiatic? (Deafening applause.) Yes, and his disciples were Asiatics, and all the agencies primarily employed for the propagation of the Gospel were Asiatic. In fact, Christianity was founded and developed by Asiatics, and in Asia. When I reflect on this, my love for Jesus becomes a hundred-fold intensified; I feel him nearer my heart, and deeper in my national sympathies. Why should I then feel ashamed to acknowledge that nationality which he acknowledged? Shall I not rather say, he is more congenial and akin to my Oriental nature, more agreeable to my Oriental habits of thought and feeling? And is it not true that an Asiatic can read the imageries and allegories of the Gospel, and its descriptions of natural sceneries, of customs and manners, with greater interest, and a fuller perception of their force and beauty, than Europeans? (Cheers.) In Christ we see not only the exaltedness of humanity, but also the grandeur of which Asiatic nature is suspectible. To us Asiatics, therefore, Christ is doubly interesting, and his religion is entitled to our peculiar regard as an altogether Oriental affair. The more this great fact is pondered, the less I hope will be the antipathy and hatred of European Christians against Oriental nationalities, and the greater the interest of the Asiatics in the teachings of Christ. And thus in Christ, Europe and Asia, the East and the West, may learn to find harmony and unity. (Deafening applause.)

I must therefore protest against that denationalization which is so general among native converts to Christianity. (Cheers.) With the religion of their heathen forefathers, they generally abandon the manners and customs of their country, and with Christianity they embrace the usages of Europeans; even in dress and diet they assume an affected air of outlandishness, which estranges them from their own countrymen. They deliberately and voluntarily cut themselves off from native society as soon as they are baptized, and, as an inevitable consequence, come to contract a sort of repugnance to everything Oriental, and an enthusiastic admiration for everything European. (Hear, hear.) They seem to be ashamed of their country and their nationality. They forget that Christ, their master, was an Asiatic, and that it is not necessary in following him to make themselves alien to their country or race. I sincerely beseech them not to confound the spirit of Christianity with the fashions of Western civilization. May they aspire to the glory of following the example of their great master, who, though he inculcated catholic truth for all mankind, was not ashamed to live and die a simple and poor Asiatic. (Cheers.)

13 / NON-WESTERN FORMS OF EVANGELISM

It was not only in movements outside the Church that distinctive adaptations of Christianity took place. They were also found, although to a more limited extent, within the Church, oft times to the dismay of missionaries from the West. On the whole, the Westerners succeeded in remaining at the helm of the churches they had formed until well into the twentieth century. But where strong national churches were in alliance with independent political power, Western control could not be exercised very effectively, and hence it was in such situations that distinctive expressions of Christianity were most likely to appear.

An example of this type of situation was the Church in Madagascar, which grew up under the sponsorship of the royal house of that country. The rulers of the island had at first allowed missionaries into the country, and then turned against them and expelled them. The new Church was subjected to severe persecutions; over 10 per cent of its members were executed. But eventually, as it became clear that Christianity was spreading rather than dying under persecution, the policy changed again, and with the accession of a new queen in 1868, Christianity became the official religion of the country. There soon appeared a national Church which, though it accepted guidance from English missionaries, also had a strong sense of its own identity and developed its own forms of life. Under royal patronage there emerged new forms of missionary outreach which bore the stamp of traditional Malagasy life. Several of the new churches of the non-Western world have carried on extensive mission work, but none has equaled in variety, indigeneity, or quantity the missions of the Church of Madagascar.

The Official Evangelists of Madagascar

In 1868 Ranavalona II began her long reign. . . . She early declared an intention to "rest my kingdom upon God." And after a period of instruction from Malagasy pastors she and her Prime Minister were both baptized. In 1869 she ordered the burning of the royal idols since they no longer represented the religious convictions upon which her government was based. . . . Although the Queen stated clearly that everyone was free to attend church or not, she did insist that all burn their idols and there was a general assumption on the part of the people that they would follow the example of their Queen in becoming Christian. Throughout Imerina [the central province] churches were quickly constructed and the natural leaders of the communities were chosen as pastors. Before the burning of the idols in 1869 there were 37,000 Christians in the country; at the end of 1870 there were 250,000. The number of native pastors increased during 1870 from a little over a thousand to 10,405. This was a national movement leaving little room for personal decisions and quite beyond the control of the missionaries. Some of them complained vigorously about the lack of freedom in this type of church growth. "The State Church in Madagascar is less tolerant than that of Turkey, Spain, or England," said one. "I have often thought," wrote another, "that we are expected to preach not the Gospel of Jesus Christ according to the New Testament, but the Gospel according to the Prime Minister." Yet technically the church was not a state church. It had no position in the constitution. There was official freedom of religion and there was not meant to be any discrimination against non-Christians in public functions.

What government participation there was in the work of evangelism and church growth came largely through the Palace Church. This was a unique institution. It met the traditional Malagasy expectation of a religious connection for government and yet left the church at large free from official control. It was a congregation made up of the highest nobility of the country and was under the control of the Queen and the Prime Minister. . . . Once the Palace Church was established its chief concern became the instruction and Christianizing of the people. In October, 1869, the Prime Minister, Rainilaiarivony, held a meeting of the preachers and teachers at his residence where it was decided that collections would be taken up in the Palace Church and other churches for the purpose of sending evangelists throughout the island. . . . The evangelists were accompanied by an official escort, and each one carried

From Charles W. Forman, "A Study in the Self-Propagating Church: Madagascar," In *Frontiers of the Christian World Mission Since 1938*, edited by Wilber C. Harr (New York and London: Harper and Row, Publishers, 1962), pp. 118-24, 126. Reprinted by permission of the publisher.

an official authorization and instruction for labors from the Queen. Their work has often been attacked by hostile critics. . . . And it is true, as we shall see later, that many criticisms can be directed at some of the high-handed methods of work of Palace Church evangelists. Yet a reading of the instructions which were given to the first group as they started out shows that in the original conception of their work and in their actual dispatch there was a praiseworthy concern for a true preaching of the Gospel and a real desire to help the people to whom they were sent. And there is no doubt that their services were badly needed in a time when churches were going up on every hand but there was no one to preach. . . .

This first group of evangelists had had no regular training and could have had only the most rudimentary knowledge of Christianity. Yet the government is hardly to be blamed for using such workers since the missionaries had already been sending out Malagasy evangelists who could not have been much better prepared. More fully trained workers were being developed and the Palace Church was quick to make use of them as soon as they were available. The missionaries had established a training college in 1869, and when the first group of students was about to complete its course in 1873 the government announced suddenly that the ten men of highest rank in the student body were to be employed as emissaries of the Palace Church. Again it was the Prime Minister, Rainilaiarivony, who was responsible for the action. The men selected for the service were all nobles and therefore liable to unpaid service of the Queen under the feudal system. . . . A solemn farewell service was organized by the Prime Minister for their departure in April, 1874, and they were given a kind of official accreditation to the authorities of the regions into which they went. There was considerable uncertainty as to how their work would fit in with the already established work of missions and churches in the provincial cities. Fortunately they were all men of ability and had been well trained by the missionaries, so they worked effectively and amicably with others in the common task. . . . After a five-year period the first ten were recalled to Tananarive, where they were given high positions in government service, and their places were taken by men of not such high standing, who often proved unequal to the task before them. From time to time in the reports sent by the missionaries to London there appeared complaints against church workers who were recalcitrant or even immoral but who could not be put out of their positions because they were in the employ of the Palace Church and had powerful protectors in the capital. There were stories of people being "thrashed to church" and on occasion Palace Church evangelists were known to order the policemen to bring people to church. One evangelist ruled his district with an iron hand and, in the missionary's opinion, ruined it. Naturally when evangelists had such prestige, it was not unknown for rogues to pose as emissaries of the Palace Church in order to secure the best hospitality of a village for a weekend or a period of weeks. T. T. Matthews, who worked just beyond the borders of Imerina in the province of Vonizongo, tells of one such imposter. When he was called upon to give a sermon he announced that he would preach from the fortieth chapter of Matthew. When the local people expostulated with him that there were not forty chapters in Matthew he disdainfully replied, "I don't know anything about your village Bibles. I'm going by the capital Bibles."

The growth of the church was fostered not only by the official evangelists sent out from the Palace Church but also by the evangelistically-minded officials representing the government in different parts of the country. Although the Queen had said clearly that there was to be freedom to pray or to stay at home, zealous officials wanting to prove their loyalty often brought pressure upon their subjects to follow the Queen's example. In Imerina itself the general acceptance of Christianity was carried out fairly rapidly after the Queen became Christian and ordered all idols burned. In the rest of the island the Merina people who had moved out of their homeland in connection with trade or government soon followed the same example. But among the other peoples over whom the Hova [the ruling class] ruled there was no such immediate and general acceptance of Christianity. Accordingly the chief efforts made by evangelistically-minded officials took place in the territories outside Imerina where there were large populations still untouched by the Church. Sometimes the governors sent out to the provinces were seriously Christian and did their best to lead the people rather than drive them in the direction of Christianity. For example, Rainiseheno, who was appointed governor of Betsileo in 1869, as much, it is said, for his goodness and piety as for his intelligence and ability, had a great desire to advance the kingdom of Christ among the Betsileo. He frequently preached in town or in the countryside and took general oversight over all the churches in the neighborhood of Fianarantsoa. One Christian remarked about him, "Each of our town churches has a pastor and the governor is father and mother to us all." Under his tutelage the Hova Christians who had shown complete apathy with regard to the conversion of the Betsileo changed radically and came to feel that their "heart's desire and prayer to God," as they put it, was that their fellow men who were still heathen "might be saved." Under him a majority of the church members in Fianarantsoa came to be Betsileo, though with Hova leadership.

Yet even such a governor as Rainiseheno carried the policy of requiring church attendance "to an extreme that is absolutely cruel; constraining the Betsileo to come extraordinary distances to worship at Fianarantsoa." As one of the missionaries working in the area wrote: The government's "unwise policy of forcing attendance because it cannot distinguish between things sacred and secular believing that those who will not worship as it does are rebellious prejudices the ignorant against Christianity." The Betsileo were often forced to help build churches and marched to church in troops by their chiefs. Some took church attendance as another form of required labor, *fanompoana,* under the feudal system. It is not surprising under these conditions that when the Hova rule was replaced by the French the Betsileo very largely fell away from these long-established churches in their territory.

A similar story comes from the area inhabited by the Tanosy tribe in the extreme south of the island. Hova rule did not extend very effectively far outside of the headquarters of that territory, Fort Dauphin, but within the area they ruled the Hovas required Christianity. A church was established when two evangelists arrived in 1880. Church attendance was obligatory and after attendance for six Sundays a person was baptized. If services were missed the offender would have to stand with a heavy rice bowl or Bible on his head as the congregation filed past him. In one government church of the area it was the practice to give out gin to enliven the singing. For a time there was an unscrupulous governor in Fort Dauphin who, though he went to church regularly and required the people to go also, helped himself to jewels from the royal tombs. He committed suicide when an investigation was begun. He was followed by a more serious-minded Christian, Andriamarovony. . . .

The combination of evangelistic officials and official evangelists was a thoroughly indigenous form of missionary activity of the Merina Christians, expressing something of the traditional unity which they had known between religion and every phase of community life. There was nothing about the system which was copied from the [foreign] missionaries. In fact the missionaries were in a peculiar position in relation to this type of evangelism. They found themselves opposed to such methods in principle. They might easily have broken with the whole system and have attacked it, bringing a fatal division among the Christian forces. But there had been growing up among them a policy favoring the development of the indigenous church of the country rather than the copying of Western Christianity . . . , and they wisely refrained from any sharp break with the expressions of the church life of the land. Rather, they worked within the system and through brotherly exhortation tried to Christianize it as much as possible.

14 / THE INVOLVEMENT OF CHRISTIANITY IN TRADITIONAL SOCIAL STRUCTURES

As the Church introduced from the West took form in Africa and Asia, it had to find an acceptable way of living with other social groups. Sometimes it was a matter of separated coexistence, the Church living as an isolated community alongside of and outside of the traditional society. Africa early provided numerous examples of this in the colonies of freed slaves and orphans which grew up around the missionaries. They had no relation to the indigenous societies within whose areas they were found, and the indigenous chieftains exercised no authority over them. In some places the missionaries withdrew all converts into this kind of "Christian village" even though they were neither ex-slaves nor orphans.

At other times the mission was established within the old society. This situation naturally produced much greater interaction between the old and the new. The patterns of Church and mission were modified by the patterns of traditional life, and vice versa. Africa also provided early examples of this kind of development, none of which was more striking than that of Buganda. This powerful kingdom, which forms the nucleus of the present Uganda, came into early contact with Christianity through the explorer Henry M. Stanley. On his expedition across the continent Stanley spent some time in Buganda and was impressed by its ruler, Mutesa. He promised Mutesa that he would see to it that missionaries were sent to teach him all that he wanted to know about European beliefs and technology. On his return to Europe Stanley made an appeal for missionaries. The Church Missionary Society from England was the first to respond, and close behind came the White Fathers from France.

Church and Political Forms in Buganda

Once they had been in the country for a year or two, the position of the missionaries was very different from that of Stanley or Speke, for the explorers had been birds of passage, while the missionaries became residents. Some decision had then to be taken by the Baganda [the people of Buganda]—and it was no less a decision for being unconscious—about the possibility of assimilating the newcomers into the traditional . . . hierarchical society. There were only a few missionaries, so that room could be found for them near the top of the hierarchy without swamping the Baganda who were already there. Moreover a mission station with its main house and surrounding outhouses was singularly like the enclosures which important Baganda chiefs maintained near the capital. It was not therefore surprising that as early as 1879, the C. M. S. missionary, Wilson, was accepted into the inner councils of the chiefs, originally on an occasion when the Kabaka [the king] was ill. The missionaries thus became, in one very real sense at least, Baganda-type senior chiefs. One result was that they became very familiar with . . . [the] society, being as it were incorporated into it.

None of them seem to have been appointed to chieftainships as some of the Arabs and Swahilis had been—they would probably have declined if it had been suggested—but for all that they seem to have been accorded the position which senior chiefs traditionally enjoyed. "Kakumba," wrote Ashe, "always took much interest in our teaching, and was very fond of coming to see us. After a time his master died, and he told us that he wished to come and serve, i.e., 'senga' us. This we allowed. Now people only go to 'senga.' i.e., serve, a chief or person of authority in the country, and our allowing young men and boys to stay at the Mission gave the chiefs, who were always listening to the slanders of our Arab enemies and others, the impression that we wished to gain a position of power and influence in the country by attaching a number of followers to ourselves." This was a natural deduction by the chiefs, which if wrong in its imputation of motive, was correct in its assessment of probable consequence. The missionaries certainly gathered around them a band of personal followers, a clientage, similar to those around the indigenous senior chiefs. . . .

From D. A. Low, *Religion and Society in Buganda, 1875-1900* (Kampala: East African Institute of Social Research, n.d.), pp. 5-11. Reprinted by permission of the publisher.

One of the chief reasons for the fairly extensive interest displayed in the missionaries' teaching among the members of the political hierarchy relates to the important point that in Buganda the only ladder to power was the political one; it was open to those with the necessary ability to climb it—there were very few hereditary offices—so that competition was intense and every conceivable advantage was eagerly sought after. It is notable that the keenest adherents of the missionaries were drawn from the younger generation at the court who were beginning to place their feet on the lower rungs of the political ladder. May they not, for instance, have been struck with the remarkable position at Mutesa's court accorded to Dallington Mufta, the U. M. C. A. boy from Zanzibar, whom Stanley had left behind to teach Mutesa Christianity, and who had become enviably associated with Mutesa's "foreign policy," merely because of his acquaintance with the white men's religion and his ability to write letters to them for the Kabaka?

Once allegiance however had been settled—whatever the motive— then, as with the traditional religion, there was an appeal to the highest motives which men possessed, and initiation by teaching, by apprenticeship, and by baptism took place. In the early years the ebb and flow of interest in the missionaries coincided with the shifts in the Kabaka's attitude towards them. But gradually some few Baganda were ready to persist in their association with the missionaries through periods when the Kabaka frowned. The point was subsequently reached when personal allegiance was in its ultimate form transferred to some considerable extent from the missionaries themselves to the Christ of whom they preached. . . . Because by 1885 the new Kabaka, Mwanga, was issuing them [the Christians] with commands that violated their Christian consciences, the conflict soon became open, with the inevitable result that the Christians involved were treated as traitors to traditional authority and were condemned to death as ordinary criminals.

Mwanga did eventually in 1888 try to exterminate the Christians by marooning them on an island in Lake Victoria. He failed, and thereby signalised his fatal mistake. For he had persecuted and therefore frightened the Christians, but had not destroyed them, and so the survivors closed in upon themselves in self-defence. . . .

During 1889, the Christians recovered their coherence, with the result that finally there emerged the [for Buganda] wholly new . . . institution—the religious party—an institution conceived in the missionaries' clientage, born of the need for self-defence, and weaned as an exclusive group amid the tribulations of exile. Because they were former adherents of the missionaries, they knew well the former C. M. S. missionary, now turned arms trader, Charlie Stokes. The major fact by March 1890 was that the Christian party—Roman Catholics and Protestants in coalition—armed by Stokes, fought their way back to power, and gained control of the traditional political system, in battle. This victory of a single group in the state was followed in the traditional manner by a clean sweep of the unsuccessful from their offices, and their replacement by the new leaders—of the Christian party. . . .

It is not altogether false to call this a Christian revolution. It obviously was in personnel; but also in some wider respects. At all events the Kabaka's autocratic powers were substantially reduced, and the mystique which had surrounded him was notably attenuated. Lugard's treaty of December 1890 was agreed to by the Kabaka and Chiefs of Buganda; previous to the Christian revolution the word of the Kabaka would have been sufficient. All this was doubtless due to the plain fact that Mwanga was not his own master any longer, and was indeed little more than the puppet of the Christian leaders. But it had a further consequence, for the Kabaka lost his arbitrary power over life and death —the power to maim, to ravage and to execute. There was, it would seem, as a result of the Christian victory, a real change in the value attached by the Baganda to human life. . . .

But just as the Christian-Mohammedan coalition of 1888 had broken up under a struggle for power, so in 1890 the Catholic-Protestant coalition began to break up in a further struggle for power. In the end, two years later, the more powerful Roman Catholics attacked the weaker Protestants, but were checked and then defeated by Captain Lugard, the agent of the Imperial British East Africa Company. Neither Lugard nor the subsequent British Imperial administration would allow the Protestants to have sole power in Buganda, and areas were parcelled out amongst the Protestants (who received the largest portion), the Roman Catholics, and even the Mohammedans. . . .

Here then, are the origins of the otherwise curious interaction in the Baganda of the Christian and the traditional. Christianity in Buganda had both absorbed some of the traditional, and been absorbed by it. So it proceeded. Having been fought on religious lines the wars deepened people's ostensible attachment to the creeds for which they had avowedly fought. Disturbed conditions making for the relatively easy entrance of new ideas into the minds of larger numbers of people were created, and with the appointment of Christian chiefs many more Baganda will have been obliged to look to Christian leaders than can have come into contact with Christian missionaries. And following the firm capture of the political hierarchy by the Christians, it must have been obvious to many Baganda that if they were to rise to positions of importance within the state, there was no chance of doing so unless they became recognised adherents of one religious party or another. That such a thought would have been correct is suggested by the land allotment lists drawn up under the 1900 Agreement. From a selective investigation it would appear that very few who were not baptised Roman Catholics or Protestants or circumcised Mohammedans were allotted more than two or three square miles of land. All the well-known Christian leaders received substantially more. This suggests that, once the Christians had gained control of the political hierarchy, not merely was the character of its authority altered, but those who were not in communion with the Christians who were in control, or with the recognised minority—the Mohammedans—found themselves "detribalised," that is, out of accord with current tribal authorities. If they wished to become "retribalised," then they had to join one of the religious parties. So that the natural traditional tendency to belong to the tribe provided, once the tribe had (as it were) been reconstituted, a powerful impetus towards conversion to Christianity. This is, of course, not the whole story, for the missionaries could still, and in fact did, insist upon a relatively high standard of Christian understanding and Christian living, before admitting to baptism or confirmation. What is more, if any indication is sought of the genuineness of much of this great movement into the church, it is to be found in the fact that the Uganda Church was at the time a missionary church spreading far and wide into neighbouring areas. But there remains the truth that Christianity had become respectable, even if—as was certainly true—it was in many instances being genuinely lived out.

15 / NEW PATTERNS FOR THE APPROPRIATION OF CHRISTIANITY

The Western missionaries were by no means always unwitting participants in or unremitting opponents of the modification of Christianity in the non-Western environment. Especially as time went on and missionaries learned to appreciate more the cultures into which they penetrated, there was a growing tendency for them to encourage indigenous variations of Christian life and action. Some of the early twentieth-century missionaries in Africa such as Edwin W. Smith, Bruno Gutmann, and, more recently, Placide Tempels, proved to be most devoted champions of the traditional forms of African life, and in other areas too Westerners took a great interest in indigenization.

An outstanding example of missionary encouragement of new patterns of Christianity is the activity of German missionaries in northeast New Guinea. There the Church spread very rapidly during the first half of the twentieth century. But it spread only after one man, Christian Keysser, had developed ways of relating the Christian faith to the traditional life of the people. Keysser devoted a great deal of attention to the indigenization of the process of Christian conversion and, through his intimate knowledge of the folkways, created ceremonies for conversion which were meaningful in the cultural context of that area. In the following passage some of the ceremonies are described by an eyewitness.

Conversion Ceremonies in New Guinea

The people of Mount Hagen in Central New Guinea had been hearing the Gospel for four years. Their manner of life had been completely changed. People came in crowds to church services; every Sunday there would be between three and four thousand of them there, sometimes even more. Everything pointed to the moment of decision having now come. The subject was discussed with the people, and especially with the chiefs. A great festival was planned to take place on a certain day. Eight tribes were invited to take part in it.

On the appointed day, the people came streaming in from every direction, and assembled at our airport. About 18,000 were present. This first day was wholly given up to the demonstration of heathenism. Each tribe organized itself and carried out its own dances. It was an overwhelming spectacle. The whole airport was a sea of men in movement. Dancing went on throughout the whole day until the evening. The reader may ask himself what all this has to do with the conversion of a tribe. The answer is that, according to Papuan psychology, nothing can be robbed of its power until it has first been put into execution. If we are intending to put away heathenism, an opportunity must first be given to show what heathenism really is.

On the second day the people came back, and grouped themselves by tribes round a high pulpit. First of all the people sang a Christian hymn; then a missionary mounted the pulpit, prayed, and delivered a short address. . . .

The various tribes were represented by their chieftains. At this point

From C. F. Vicedom, *Church and People in New Guinea* (New York: Association Press; London: Lutterworth Press, 1961), pp. 17-22. Reprinted by permission of the Lutterworth Press.

the chiefs, one after the other, approached the pulpit. Each had a number of small pieces of wood in his hand. Each addressed his people roughly in the following manner: "See, my people; here I have in my hand a piece of wood. Its name is war. You know how we used to fight with one another. No one could go anywhere without fear. We could not sleep at night for pricking up our ears at every sound. Since the Word of God came to us, peace has returned. Now for the first time we know how pleasant life can be. Now what is your choice? Shall we go back to fighting as we used to do, or shall we continue to live in peace?" The people answered: "We choose peace. We promise never to go to war again." The chief continued, "See now, as I throw away this piece of wood, so we cast war away. From henceforth everyone among us shall live in safety. We will not kill any more!" The people responded, "We will not kill any more."

The chief resumed, "Here I have a stick called sorcery. We used to be even more afraid of sorcery than we were of war. If anyone was ill, he at once said to himself 'I am bewitched.' If any misfortune happened, it was the sorcerer who had been at work. If our crops did not prosper, we attributed it to sorcery. Sorcery is the mother of fear. God's Word has driven out sorcery. No one speaks about it any more. When we are ill, God heals us by means of medicines. Now what is your choice? Shall we keep sorcery, or shall we decide not to put up with it any longer?" The people replied: "We have learned to pray. Never again will we have anything to do with sorcery." The chief: "See now, as I throw this piece of wood away—away with sorcery! Henceforth sorcery shall not be practised here." The people: "henceforth sorcery shall not be practised here."

The chief: "My next piece of wood has to do with something that concerns women. You know what you did in old times when you had a baby. If you didn't like the baby, or if you were afraid of the work that it would cause, you did away with it. We men were often angry about this. To how many quarrels did it lead! God's Word tells us that it is God who gives us children. Now what is your choice? Do you intend to go on getting rid of the little ones as you used to do? Or are you prepared to bring them up as a gift from God?" The women: "We will obey God. We will bring up the children and not get rid of them." The chief: "See now, as I cast away this piece of wood, so we cast away child-murder from us. From now on no child shall be killed among us." The women: "From now on no child shall be killed among us."

In this way all the sins that were common among the people were worked through—theft, adultery, the worship of ancestors and so on. By the time that all the chiefs had said their say, it was already noon. Next came the second part of the day's business—turning to God. Once again a missionary mounted the pulpit. He held a new net in his hand, showed it to the people and said, "This net is now fresh and clean. It is also quite empty. In the same way your hearts are empty. You have shaken out all your sins. Nothing evil is left in them. But do you think that they will remain empty?" "No" cried out the whole assembly. "Will it not be as in the parable, where the devil finds a house, empty, swept and put in order? Unless something else enters into your hearts, the devil will find his way back again."

"We wish God to enter into our hearts."

"Very well; but you must first commit yourselves to God."

Near the pulpit was a short wooden pole firmly fixed in the earth.

"See, God is here in the midst of you. God is here like this pole which stands firm and strong before you. No one can pull it up. No one can overturn it. It stands quite firm. In the same way God will never leave you. In this God you can completely trust. The man who wishes that God should enter into his empty heart must now commit himself to him."

Once again, each chief carried out this ceremony for the people of his own tribe. . . .

This part of the ceremonies also lasted several hours. The missionaries imagined that at last everything was at an end; but they were mistaken. As the missionary who was in the pulpit came down, the people told him that their promise was not yet fully ratified. "Come," they said. Without his knowledge a small garden-plot had been prepared at a little distance. Then they said to the missionary, "When we are making a promise that must in no circumstances be broken, the two partners must plant a little tree together. Here are the seedlings. You must plant one of them in the earth with each of the chiefs." This, too, was a solemn ceremony. When it was finished, the people were satisfied that everything had been done in due and proper order.

It is clear that "conversion of a tribe" does not lead on automatically to "baptism of a tribe." It only makes it possible for the individual to be baptized without in consequence being driven out from the fellowship of his people. The baptism of a tribe may be spread out over a long period, and decades may pass before the last individual has finally made his decision. Since, however, the whole tribe has declared its will to be Christian, the Christian group from the date of its formation can take the lead in the affairs of the tribe.

CHRISTIAN SOCIAL SERVICE

16 / THE MISSION SCHOOL

Beyond the strictly religious activities conducted by Christians in the non-Western world, there came in the nineteenth century a growing stress on Christian social service. In earlier times there had been scattered examples of social service of one kind or another offered in conjunction with missionary labors, but most Christian service had been provided only to those within the Church. No specialized service programs for non-Christians had ever been established. Such programs began to appear, however, in the first half of the nineteenth century, and during the twentieth century they became the predominant form of missionary work.

First in importance as well as in time came the educational program. It is through Christian schools and colleges that Christianity has made its major contribution to and impact on the non-Western world. In Africa the great bulk of the education provided until now has been that given by mission schools. The same was long true in the South Pacific. In Asia the Western missions did not play so dominant a part, yet even in a country like India, the majority of students were educated in Christian schools during the greater part of the nineteenth century.

The most notable and effective proponent of education as a form of missionary endeavor was Alexander Duff, a Scotsman who sailed for India in 1829. He was the first missionary sent by the Church of Scotland, and he determined to explore possibilities for new forms of service. After a time of exploration he decided on the project of educating the leaders of Hindu society in Western knowledge, and in the English language, for he believed that Indian languages were not adequate to convey Western science. It was his expectation that Western science would release students from their Hindu beliefs and open them to Christian faith. Christian service thus became a strong force for Westernization. His educational proposal was regarded as foolhardy by many. But in spite of this, the young man, only twenty-four years of age, announced that he would open an institution for the higher education of the Hindu community with the lessons given in English and with instruction in Christianity. On July 12, 1830, in Duff's own words, "the greatest missionary experiment India has ever witnessed was begun." The following is his description of the inauguration of the school and of the reception it was accorded.

Alexander Duff's Experiment in Western Education

A tolerably sized hall in an old building in the central part of the native town—once occupied as a Hindu College, and latterly as a chapel by "Hindu Unitarians" or Pantheists, was hired for the purpose. All the necessary preparations in fitting it for educational purposes having been completed by Monday the 12th July, a note was forwarded on the evening of that day to a native of rank and influence, who had expressed himself favourable to our design; stating, that on the following morning we should attend at the intended school. On Tuesday, at his recommendation, five young men made their appearance. With these chiefly, through an interpreter, we had a long and pleasing colloquy. They went away expressing themselves highly gratified. The tidings they communicated to their friends and neighbours. On Wednesday twenty more appeared. The most of these, too, retired with the most favourable impressions. On Thursday, the number of *additional* candidates amounted to *eighty*. So that, without public notice or advertisement of any description, the hall, which only held about one hundred and twenty, was completely filled in *three* days.

On Friday, it was our intention to examine, arrange, and classify, but were prevented from so doing by the appearance of upwards of *two hundred new* applicants. These assembled in the back court; and in their petitions were so clamorous and importunate, that after struggling in vain to explain and pacify, we found it utterly impossible to proceed. Judging from the exceeding earnestness of the entreaties, that instead of having to solicit the attendance of any as a favour, hundreds must be refused for want of sufficient accommodation, it was announced that a selection would be made; and, that in order to secure the greatest decorum and regularity, every application must be made in writing; and accompanied, if possible, by a special recommendation from some respectable native or European gentleman. . . .

Throughout the whole progress of these preparatory arrangements, the excitement among the natives continued unabated. They pursued us along the streets. They threw open the very doors of our palankeen; and poured in their supplications with a pitiful earnestness of countenance that might have softened a heart of stone. In the most plaintive and pathetic strains, they deplored their ignorance. They craved for "Eng-

From Alexander Duff, *India, and India Missions* (Edinburgh: John Johnstone, 1839), pp. 525-27, 532-42, 557-59, 573-74.

lish reading," "English knowledge." They constantly appealed to the compassion of an "Ingraji" or Englishman; addressing us in the style of Oriental hyperbole, as "the great fathomless ocean of all imaginable excellencies," for having come so far to teach poor ignorant Bengalis. And then, in broken English, some would say, "Me good boy, oh take me"; others, "Me poor boy, oh take me"; some, "Me want read your good books, oh take me"; others, "Me know your commandments, Thou shalt have no other gods before me, oh take me"; and many, by way of final appeal, "oh take me, and I pray for you." And, even after the final choice was made, such was the continued press of new candidates, that it was found absolutely necessary to issue small written tickets for those who had succeeded; and to station two men at the outer door to admit only those who were of the selected number. . . .

The plan or mode of tuition adopted was what has been termed "the intellectual system"; which has been brought to such perfection by those distinguished educational philanthropists, Mr. Wood of Edinburgh, and Mr. Stow of Glasgow; subject, of course, to such peculiar modifications in the arrangements and details, as the change of circumstances obviously demanded. This is the natural and true system; suited to the condition and capacity of rational beings. It was beyond all debate the strenuous and unabated prosecution of this Indianized modification of the intellectual or mental development system of instruction, which, under the direction of Divine Providence, so speedily caused the infant Institution to outpeer all its predecessors in the estimation both of natives and of Europeans. . . .

At first, even the most advanced of the boys and young men appeared to possess little or no characteristic intelligence. If, on distinctly pronouncing such a simple sentence as this—"The sun shines"—it was asked, What is it that shines? the question would be answered by a vacant unintelligent stare. They had read something, but, to attend to the import of what they read, or exercise the least degree of thought upon it, was a practice to them wholly unknown. Still, there was nothing to discourage. Having ourselves experienced all the horrors of the dull old mechanical system during the earlier years spent in school, and being able even now to realize the impress of that unbounded joy which filled the soul, when first emancipated from its thraldom, and made to feel conscious of the possession of at least some small portion of reason, we readily persuaded ourselves that, under a system of tuition still more imperfect. it was almost impossible for the youth assembled before us to make a different exhibition. Instead, therefore, of upbraiding them for their apparent stupidity, we were naturally led to cheer and encourage, warmly expressing our conviction that the fault was not theirs if they appeared to such disadvantage, cheerfully ascribing their present state to causes over which they had no control, and strongly assuring them that, by persevering diligence, their progress might not only be sure, but rapid. Sooner than could well be anticipated were our expectations realized. Scarcely had a week elapsed, when the state of things assumed a decided change of aspect. Forwardness of manner became respectful: irregularity of habit acknowledged some rule: sluggishness of movement was quickened: the unfixed tendency of thought seemed more stayed: fickleness and levity of conduct settled down into greater sobriety: aimlessness of effort began to be directed to a purpose; and passive indolence of mind was aroused into activity. . . .

This was the time for the *formal* introduction of that prime branch of knowledge, without which all education is more than defective. . . .

It was at once freely confessed that the subject was not without difficulties. But, to the shame of our countrymen, it must be told that these difficulties, though not perhaps originated, had been increased a hundredfold by the base and treacherous proceedings of Britons bearing the Christian name. . . . Instead of fearlessly appealing to the Bible as the fountainhead of all sound principle in legislation, jurisprudence, and religion, their grand scheme of policy was, by every possible artifice, treacherously to conceal their faith; and by threats of pains and penalties, wholly to keep back from view and to suppress the great standard of that faith. . . . From the educational system pursued in every Government seminary, and every Institution patronized by Government officials (apart from the elementary mission-schools), the Bible was systematically excluded by rules as rigorous and inviolable as those that regulate the maintenance of a strict quarantine in warding off the pestilence or the plague. Hence it happened that the odium, originally excited towards the Bible as some unknown evil of portentous magnitude, instead of being diminished, was unreasonably enhanced. . . .

The substance and form of address assumed, as nearly as possible, was the following: "My young friends, one great object of my coming hither, is to convey to you, *all* the European knowledge I possess myself —*literary, scientific,* and *religious.* You, too, have vast store-houses of knowledge, such as it is. And I cannot but confess the humiliating fact, that your ancestors were comparatively learned and civilized, when mine were nothing better than ignorant painted barbarians, who, somewhat like your Bengal tigers, ranged at large over the jungly forests; or like your Himalayan bears, roved wild over the mountains. But times are changed now, and we, their descendants, have changed with the times. We have now become civilized, and possess vast treasures of learning which we reckon worthy of being communicated to others. Of this, you yourselves prove that you are not ignorant, by the desire which you have manifested to acquire our language; and, through it, our learning. As there is a book—the Vedas—which you reckon the fountainhead of all your best knowledge; so there is a book—the Bible—which we esteem the fountainhead of all our best knowledge. . . .

The books were then opened. The Lord's Prayer was distinctly read and explained, paragraph by paragraph. It was thenceforth used every morning, as a solemn form of adoration and prayer, before entering on the duties of the day. From that time forward, the first hour was devoted to the reading of a portion of the Bible. . . .

The conversation being conducted, partly in Bengali and partly in English, a few days after the commencement of our labours, it happened that the word "rain" occurred in the lesson of one of the junior classes. In the course of ordinary interrogation, the question was put, What is rain? It was replied, "Water from the sky." Has it been produced by the sky itself? "No." How then has it been formed? "Oh," said one, with the smartness and self-possession so characteristic of Hindu youth. "Do you not know that yourself?" I think I do, said the master; but my present object is to find out whether you know it. "Well," remarks another, with an air of manifest satisfaction. "I'll tell you. It comes from the trunk of Indra's elephant." Indeed, said I, that is a new theory of the origin of rain, which I did not know before; and I should now like to be informed on what evidence it is founded. "All I can say about it," responded he, "is, that my *Guru,* (or religious teacher), told me so." But your *Guru* must have some reason for telling you so. Did he ever see the elephant himself? "Oh no, how could he? The elephant is wrapped up in the cloud, as in a covering; and no one can, therefore, see it with his own eyes." How then came the *Guru* to know that the elephant was there at all? "To be sure," said he, "because the Shastra says so." Now I understand the matter; You have asserted that the rain comes from the trunk of Indra's elephant, simply because the *Guru* has told you that this is the account contained in the Shastra? "Certainly: for, though I have never seen it with my own eyes, yet I believe it is there; because the

Guru has told me that the Shastra says so; and what the Shastra says must be true."

At the early period at which this conversation took place, tyro as we were in our knowledge of the *minutiae* of Hinduism, we were not in the least aware of the existence of such a theory at all. Hence the *reality* of our own surprise when it was first announced. Subsequently we learned that either the boy or the Guru had been under a slight mistake. The shastra-theory of the cause of a specific meteorological phenomenon, had been expanded into a theory of the origin of rain in general. Strictly speaking, it is what we term a "waterspout," which in the Shastra is declared to be a violent jet from the trunk of the elephant on which Indra, the god of the firmament, is represented as riding when traversing his aerial domains. This slight mistake, however, very little affected the *mode* and *manner* of the mental process of arriving at the conclusion which followed.

True to our original predetermined design, we did not choose *directly* to contradict the Shastra, by casting ridicule on the alleged theory, as palpably absurd; or branding it as absolutely false, the manifest corruption of a mythological fable. Instead of this we simply remarked to the boys that the theory which their Guru had taught was very different, indeed, from that which our *Guru* had taught us in Scotland. And now that we had learnt from them their theory on the subject, it was asked whether they would not like to hear ours, and so have an opportunity of comparing the two together. Nothing would delight them more. Their attention was then directed to a very simple phenomenon. It was asked, In boiling your rice what is observed to rise from the vessel? "Smoke or vapour." When a dry lid is held for some time over it, what effect is produced? "It gets wet." What makes it wet? "The smoke or vapour." True; and when it gets very, very wet, does all the vapour continue to stick to it? "No; it falls off in drops." Very good. What then would you say of the vapour itself, that it is dry or wet? "Wet, sure enough." And whence can the wet vapour proceed? "It can only be from the water in the vessel." Is the vapour a different kind of substance from the water? "No." Why think you so? "Because when it gathers on the lid we see it turn into water again." So you conclude that the vapour is just a part of the water in the vessel? "Yes." . . . The attention was next directed to the application of all this. The pupils were referred to a very familiar phenomenon in Bengal. After a heavy fall of rain on the heated ground, when the morning sun darts from a cloudless horizon, they were asked what they had been accustomed to witness? "Great vapours." It was then brought out, at some length, in an interrogatory form, that these vapours consisted of water exhaled by the heat of the sun; like the vapour separated from the water in the vessel, by the heat of the fire; that these vapours, ascending, impinged on the cold, upper strata of the atmosphere, exactly as the vapour from the water in the vessel did upon the cold lid; and that, becoming there condensed and accumulated beyond what the atmosphere could uphold, the whole fell back again upon earth, in multiplied drops of rain. Such, added we, is the simple theory of the origin of rain, which we once learnt from our Guru in Scotland. . . .

Our plan, therefore, was not first to plant and rear the tree of literary and scientific knowledge, and afterwards to graft upon it a scion from the stem of Christianity. Such a graft would prove but a sickly exotic on an uncongenial stock; and, however often renewed, could never flourish and produce good fruit. Neither was it our plan to plant and rear the tree of religious knowledge, and afterwards, by some process of "budding," attempt to force the young tendrils of literary and scientific knowledge to sprout therefrom. Such unnatural forcing could only produce what was feeble and worthless, while the violence endured would cause the parent trunk to degenerate. Religion and science have each its own independent seed; and why should not each be sown and take independent root? But though independent in their root and growth, why should they be reared as antagonists? . . . Why should they not rather be planted and reared in happy and mutual alliance? To accomplish this was our great object.

17 / THE MISSION HOSPITAL

Second to educational work came medical work. In many areas Christian missions were the first to bring Western medicine to non-Western peoples. Specialized medical missions began with the arrival of Peter Parker in China in 1834. By the late nineteenth century considerable numbers of medical missionaries were to be found in most parts of the non-Western world. Their numbers increased greatly in the early twentieth century. The work of individual doctors led to the establishment of hospitals and even, occasionally, to medical schools. Curative efforts were supplemented by preventive medicine and public health programs. The training of nurses was in many lands a peculiarly Christian contribution.

In some of the more tightly closed Islamic areas of the Middle East medical work proved to be the principal type of Christian service that it was possible to develop. As an example of the work done in such an area we reproduce here part of the report for the year 1904 issued by Dr. Joseph Plumb Cochran, in charge of the hospital in Urumia in northwest Iran, then called Persia. In its description of the variety of classes served and the impact upon the community at large, it could well have been written about almost any mission hospital. During the latter part of the nineteenth century, when Dr. Cochran was working there, northwest Iran was still an untamed district only partially subject to the central government. The Kurds who lived in the mountains were notorious for their attacks upon villages and on travelers. Some particulars of their depredations were so well known to Dr. Cochran that they wished to put an end to him, and not long before this report was written, they had killed one of his fellow missionaries in a mountain pass, mistaking him for the doctor.

Report from Iran

There have been 574 patients treated during the year in the hospital. These, as in former years, have been from among all classes and conditions of men; from this plain, from the mountains, and from the surrounding countries. One set of men in whose treatment we took a considerable satisfaction, was a company of Kurds. Their home is in one of the wildest gorges of Kurdistan, and the chief of that place, Sutu Beg, holds undisputed sway for a long distance about it. He sent his nephew to me with a letter resembling very closely that which Naaman bore to the King of Israel. It read somewhat as follows: "Now when this letter is come unto thee, behold, I have therewith sent Kazim, my nephew, to thee, that thou mayest recover him of his troubles. Thou wilt return him soon to me that we may all rejoice in his recovery, and praise God and thee." Kazim had with him a number of other men in rank and position, all of whom were under treatment. When they are dismissed, they went away in a very happy and grateful frame of mind. . . .

At the College Commencement we graduated four medical students who had completed their course of four years. This class ranks well with others that have graduated here. All four of the young men, one a Moslem, and the other three Syrians, began practice for themselves as soon as they took diplomas, which I got the Crown Prince to indorse, as well as his chief native doctor, who boasts the title of Loghman-ul-Mamalik,

From "Report for the Year 1904" in *The Foreign Doctor. A Biography of Joseph Plumb Cochran, M.D. of Persia* by Robert E. Spear (New York: Fleming H. Revell Co., 1911), pp. 270-72. Reprinted by permission of the publisher.

or the Loghman of Kingdoms. One of these young men went to Souj Bulak, a city in the southern part of this Province. While there the cholera epidemic visited the district, and he was able to be of much service to the inhabitants because of his having been invited by the Governor to be his family physician, and having gained his confidence, he was permitted to order such reforms in the sanitary condition of the town as to make it better prepared to resist the disease. The Governor secured for this young man from the Crown Prince the title of "The Illustrious among the Physicians." As I have pointed out at other times, the mission of teaching the medical science to the young men of this nation here, and right here in their homes, is doing a great deal to remove the prejudice that existed on the part of the Mohammedan nobility towards this despised and ignorant class. They find that they are capable of high attainments, and as soon as they acquire this profession they are quick to remunerate them in elevating their social position, and taking them as their own confidential medical advisers.

In the outside medical work we have had many interesting patients. One was a gentleman of high rank from Teheran, who has been governor of two districts in this Province the last three years. He was in need of an operation for cancer, and was advised by the Tabriz physician to come here. He arrived with his wife and large retinue carriage and takhtirawans (litters). He had over one hundred horses to move his household. He engaged rooms in the city, where he kept house, and put himself under my care. The operation was successful, and he gave a very handsome fee for my services, according to the estimate of this country. I spent the first night with him, and after that saw him once or twice daily until he recovered completely and was dismissed. All through the first night, and many subsequent ones, he had four or five men sit around his bed that was spread on the floor, as usual, and knead his muscles so that he should sleep. This custom is very common among those who can afford many attendants. I have received almost weekly letters from him since his departure, and he is very grateful. His wife was a very pleasant, refined lady, and under treatment also. There have been many cases under my care among the nobility this year, rather more than common, and more than I could well attend, but it has perhaps well paid me for the trouble, because of the influence which I could exert in these homes. . . . An illustration of the other extreme of life was a woman who also came from a distance, leaving her husband and three small children in a pitiable condition with only God above and none below to care for them. The morning she left she covered the children in the stable with the dried manure used to bed the animals, and came away, as she expressed it, with "only Heaven above them, and hell under them, and their stomachs empty." The suffering of the poor sick in this country is most pitiful, and the deaths from these conditions is very heavy, especially among the children. At best the common people have only a charcoal dish under a low table with a spread over the latter, around which they gather, drawing the spread over them as far as it will cover them.

18 / CHRISTIAN SOCIAL REFORM MOVEMENTS

Christianity has frequently become involved with social reform. This has been as often true in the non-Western world as it has in the West. In fact, reformist tendencies have been accentuated by the interest of Western churchmen in introducing reforms patterned after the Christian and humanitarian standards of the West. Out of such interest came the campaign by missionaries to end the practice of sati—*the self-immolation of widows—in India, or the efforts in China to end the crippling practice of foot-binding for women.*

But Christianity was not concerned only with removing those evils which were at variance with Western practice; numerous Christian reform efforts were directed against the evils springing from the impact of Western culture. The long struggle of Christians against the slave trade in Africa was the most widely recognized and most extensive of these movements. It involved missionaries in the exploration of unopened areas, the purchasing of the freedom of slaves and the establishment of settlements for them, the creation of alternative forms of industry and commerce, and the backing of governmental prohibitions and pursuit of slavers. Less well known are the efforts of Christians in Japan to deal with the evils attendant upon the process of industrialization inspired by the West. Christianity reentered Japan at about the same time that industrialization began, and Christian Japanese were among the first to sense the problems of the new industrial proletariat. The following account of their concern is written by a young Japanese scholar.

Labor and Socialism in Japan

In the field of social work, the pioneering nature of the Christian contribution has been highly significant, and, even more than in the case of education, this contribution in social work continues to this day. In the

From Masao Takenaka, *Reconciliation and Renewal in Japan* (New York: Friendship Press, 1957), pp. 28, 36-42. Reprinted by permission of the publisher.

fall of 1956, the Japanese government was asked to name the four most outstanding leaders in the field of social work in Japanese history. The four then nominated were: Juji Ishii, founder of the Okayama Orphanage—the largest orphanage in that district: Kosuke Tomeoka, who worked in prison reform and established a reformatory; Gumpei Yamamuro, founder of the Salvation Army and social settlements and a leader in the temperance movement; and Takeo Iwahashi, the founder of the Light House in Osaka, a center for those who like himself are blind. Christians—all of them!

Another incident to show the leadership of Christians in social work came in 1926 when the government made awards to those who had contributed most to the development of social work since the Meiji era. Twenty-two out of thirty-two people receiving these awards were Christian. . . .

After the Sino-Japanese War of 1894-95, there was rapid development of thinking in support of a labor movement in Japan. It is widely recognized that the early labor and socialist movements were notably influenced by Western culture in general and Christian ethics in particular. Two streams are clearly discernible in the early socialist movement in Japan—one was developed out of dialectic materialism, the other built upon the Christian faith. The socialist movement developed through the interaction of these two groups, which sometimes cooperated and at other times were antagonistic to each other.

It was an epoch-making event when on June 25, 1897, at the Tokyo Y.M.C.A., the Association for the Formation of Labor Unions was born. In its statement of purpose this organization resolved "to maintain the rights of labor, to sustain the good tradition, to remove abuses, and to encourage the formation of unions which will unite labor." In 1898 this organization had over 1,000 members; a year later the membership had reached 5,700. Many Christians were active in the formation of this union; Sen Katayama was appointed staff secretary and a member of the publication and lecture committee; Sumio Shimada, Tomoyoshi Murai, and Isoo Abe acted as councilors. Although the organization made no explicit mention of Christianity, it implicitly accepted Christian principles. The leaders called for mutual support among laboring people and, in the interest of labor's welfare, advocated gradual and peaceful means of reform rather than sudden and violent revolution. The practical principles by which Katayama and others led the labor union movement were expressed by a statement appearing in the first issue of *The Labor World,* a monthly magazine that Katayama began in 1897. In this he said, "The policy of *The Labor World* is to manifest two mottoes: 'Labor Is Holy' and 'Union Is Power.' "

Under the leadership of the association, several unions were organized. One of these, the Iron Workers' Union, was the first labor union in the modern sense in Japan. It had 1,075 members in eleven factories when it was organized in 1897. Another union formed under the guidance of the association the following year was the Association for Reform, an organization of railroad engineers and firemen of the Japan Railway Company. Shortly after the formation of this union, the railway engineers and firemen went on strike to protest the discharge of ten persons because of their demand for higher wages. This strike ended in a victory for the labor union and a clear demonstration of organized labor's power.

The other union that was organized at this time was the Printing Workers' Union, established in 1898. The president of the union was Saburo Shimada, a Christian, a member of the Association for the Formation of Labor Unions, a champion of the temperance movement, and a crusader against licensed prostitution.

Thus in this period Christians in the labor movement, mainly through the Association for the Formation of Labor Unions, made an effort to advance the dignity of work, emphasized the necessity of mutual assistance, and helped in the organization of unions.

In addition to the practical efforts toward organizing labor unions and educating labor regarding the need for mutual assistance, there was also an urgent need for a systematic study of social problems, and in 1890 the Association for the Study of Social Problems was formed by Yujiro Miyake, Sen Katayama, Teiichi Sukuma, Tokichi Tarui, and Charles E. Garst. There were about two hundred members including people of different points of view.

Out of this group, in the fall of 1898, came the Association for the Study of Socialism, which was concerned to understand the principles of socialism and their application to Japanese society. The members met regularly at the hall of the Unitarian Society in Tokyo for lectures and discussions. Although this association also had members from various backgrounds, Christian humanists constituted its main body. Eight of the fourteen original members were associated with the Unitarian Society of Tokyo. Many from this group went to America for study and were greatly influenced there both by liberal theology and by socialism. One of the non-Christian socialists who joined in this group commented upon the Christians in the group as follows: "This association was established mainly by Christians. Although these people went to the Western countries to study Christianity, they knew at the same time the material circumstances of actual society and could not limit their studies entirely to abstract theology. Rather they sought to apply a Christian spirit to the material world."

In 1900, when Isoo Abe became the chairman of the association, the nonsocialist members withdrew, and the name was changed to the Socialist Association, reflecting a readiness to participate in an actual movement. In addition to convictions arrived at through theoretical study, other factors were influencing the members of the association to give serious consideration to the socialist creed. The constant oppression of the labor movement by the government was sharply intensified by the enactment of a new Peace Preservation Law in 1900. This law again put heavy restrictions upon the labor movement, and Katayama as a practical leader of the union movement expressed his criticism in *The Labor World:* "A strike is the means whereby labor may make its final bargain under the constitution. This is the right of labor, and if one makes an effort for this purpose, he should be permitted freedom of speech and not be suppressed by police as long as he does not threaten the life of employers nor the destruction of their property." The repressive measures of the government continued, and Katayama became an advocate of socialism. . . .

. . . While the government maintained its oppression by laws against the labor movement, there were no laws such as factory laws, employer's liability, or working men's insurance laws to guard the rights of working people. Many women and children were mercilessly employed in the factories. One document illustrates how severe was the condition for young girls temporarily employed in the cotton mills:

> Everyday working hours were never less than thirteen or fourteen hours or in some cases they even went as high as seventeen to eighteen hours. . . . The night shift involved such hard work that very few were willing to accept it; therefore, the company ordered girls who were staying in the company dormitory to go back to work after their regular day and to continue on into the next morning. In one case a girl worked for thirty-six hours without any sleep, and similar practices were not rare.

In view of the situation, those who were concerned with social reform came to realize the limitations of a fraternal unionism that aimed at the development of harmony between labor and management. They realized that political action was necessary in order to bring about a socialism that would benefit the working people and advance their total welfare. Thus, in 1901, a group of socialists who had been studying together in the association formed the Social Democratic Party. Those who founded the party were Katayama, Abe, Kinoshita, Kawakami, Nishikawa, and Kotoku, all of whom were Christians with the exception of Kotoku, who was influenced by materialistic socialism. However, again difficulty was encountered, for when they applied to the authorities for permission to promote such a party, the party was dissolved by the Minister of Home Affairs.

This party, the first of socialist parties in Japan, was not radical nor did it aim at violent methods. It was dedicated to a thoroughgoing and gradual reform of society. The declaration of the party reflected a general implicit belief in Christian humanism among its leaders. They expressed sympathy with the oppressed workers; they protested against the domination of the privileged classes; and they contended against the wide cleavage between the poor and the rich. Its spirit was one of pacifism rather than violent conflict, of gradual progressivism rather than revolution, and of lawful means rather than a disrespect for the existing laws. The positive goals laid down in the party platform expressed the ideals of democratic socialism. In its first platform the party laid out eight points that were considered to be "ideal": (1) universal brotherhood; (2) abolition of the Army and Navy and the realization of international peace; (3) abolition of class distinctions, and political and economic equality; (4) common ownership of land and capital; (5) public ownership of railways, steamships, canals, bridges, and other means of communication; (6) equitable distribution of wealth; (7) equal share of political rights by all people; and (8) complete education of all at the expense of the government.

Despite the fact that the party was dissolved by the Minister of Home Affairs, the Socialist Association continued to work on education and propaganda for socialism. In the fall of 1903, they organized the Commoner's Association, and they started a weekly journal called *Commoner's News*, which advocated socialism and took a pacifist stand against the Russo-Japanese War of 1904-05. Pressure from the government continued, however, and the Socialist Association was ordered to dissolve on November 16, 1904. In addition to government pressure, the Commoner's Association also was having problems of its own. It was having financial difficulties, and serious divisions were arising from the ideological differences between the Christian socialists and the materialistic Marxist socialists. As the external pressure became stronger, the internal difficulties increased, and the Commoner's Association finally dissolved in 1905.

After the dissolution of the Commoner's Association, the socialist camp was divided in several directions. Christian socialists like Abe, Ishikawa, and Kinoshita gathered together to publish their journal, *The New Era*. The materialistic or atheistic socialists like Yamaguchi and Nishikawa established *The Light* as their organ. Sakai started the independent magazine called *The Home Magazine*. These men not only separated but also bitterly criticized one another. . . .

As government suppression became severe, many of the prominent leaders among the Christian socialists moved to the radical left wing group. On the other hand, some withdrew from the socialist movement and retired from public life. Of the original group of Christian socialists, very few remained in the movement as Christians.

IV / THE MID-TWENTIETH CENTURY: CONFRONTATION AND SELF-ASSERTION

INTRODUCTION

As the twentieth century advanced, it became clear that non-Western Christianity was entering upon a new phase, a period of trial and test, of growing maturity and self-expression. The principal factor in bringing on the change was again the relations between East and West on the world stage. The growth of anti-Western forces in Asia and Africa forced a gradual retreat of Western power from those continents. Christianity, because of its close Western ties, was caught in the attack on the West, and the churches had to reconsider their role in Asia and Africa. In some ways the new period was more like the earlier days before the nineteenth-century avalanche of Western influence. The churches of Africa and the East, often touched with the same anti-Western feeling, began to loosen their ties to the West and to express their own character within the African and Asian environment. Both Catholics and Protestants hastened the development of indigenous leadership, displacing the Western leaders who had dominated for so long. The churches proceeded to take responsibility for their own affairs and began to speak in terms of their own selfhood. The era of the non-Western Church or, as it was more commonly designated, the indigenous Church had dawned.

The general reaction against the West expressed itself largely in terms of nationalism. Hence it was primarily in the confrontation with nationalism that Christianity was forced to work out its new place in the non-Western world. The confrontation was a complex one, for while nationalism as an anti-Western force tended to be hostile to Christianity, there were also many nationalists within the churches and many similarities between the Western inspiration of nationalism and the Western links of Christianity. The first group of selections which follows reveals something of that complexity.

The other principal path of anti-Western attack came through Communism. Here the lines were more sharply drawn, since the Communists excluded Christian believers from the ranks of their leaders. Nevertheless, something of a dialogue between Christian and Communist took place, and from it two selections are given. The final group of selections sets forth a few examples of the self-expression of the Christianity which was emerging through this period, though it needs to be recognized that much of this self-expression may also be found in the confrontations with nationalism and Communism.

THE CONFRONTATION WITH NATIONALISM

19 / CHRISTIANITY UNDER NATIONALIST ATTACK

In China the nationalist or, perhaps more precisely, the xenophobic attack on Christianity was no new development of the mid-twentieth century. The Chinese had previously expressed their antipathy to the foreigners and the revolutionary foreign religion through frequent denunciations and outbursts of violence in the nineteenth century. At certain times it seemed that wherever Christians went, they were confronted by showers of stones and curses. In some places whole towns rose in riots against the Christians. The twentieth century began with the Boxer Rebellion, which claimed the lives of perhaps as many as thirty thousand Chinese Christians and over two hundred foreign missionaries and their children.

But it was not until the 1920s that a modern type of nationalism was developed and turned against Christianity. The relation of Christianity to this nationalism was certainly ambivalent, for the two most famous nationalist leaders, Sun Yat-sen and Chiang Kai-shek, were both Christians. Yet the missionaries had benefited from extraterritoriality and the "unequal" treaties, and Christianity had been given special protection in the toleration clauses of the treaties. During the 1920s arose an anti-Christian movement which resulted in drastic reductions in the number of missionaries and in difficulties for the Chinese churches. No other land experienced quite so organized and violent an anti-Christian reaction. In India, Indonesia, and Burma during the 1930s and in Ceylon during the 1950s there were nationwide attacks on Christianity as part of the reaction against Western influence generally, but they did not reach the proportions of the movement in China. The following report comes from a Christian living in the midst of the Chinese anti-Christian movement and, while living with it, endeavoring to understand it.

The Anti-Christian Movement in China

The beginnings of the opposition first appeared when the magazine of the Y.M.C.A. . . . outlined the programme for the gathering of the World Student Christian Federation. In reply a student group in Shanghai began to prepare an anti-Christian programme, and gave notice of the organization of an Anti-Christian Students Federation

> We oppose the World Student Christian Federation because we wish to guard the happiness and welfare of humanity. . . . Capitalism in the world has gone through its stages of development, first ripening, then coming to decay. Thus it is that capitalists of all nations, British, American, Japanese, French, are afraid and try all manner of clever means to eke out their dying breath against ten thousand odds. They are therefore taking steps, one after another, to rush into China, to carry out their plans of economic exploitation. And present-day Christianity and the Christian Church are the vanguard of this exploitation. . . . The World Student Christian Federation is the progeny of present-day Christianity and the Christian Church. They are preparing to call together Christians from all over the world, and to hold a Conference on 4th April at Tsing Hua College, Peking. What they intend to discuss is nothing more than such schemes as how to uphold capital and how to extend capitalism in China. We regard this conference as a conference of robbers, humiliating and polluting our youth, cheating our people, and stealing our economic resources. Therefore following the dictates of our hearts, we are organizing this Federation to declare war upon it.
>
> Students! Young men! Workers! Who among us does not know the sins of the capitalist? Who among us is blind to his heartless cruelty? What can we do but rise and oppose them when we see with our own eyes these bloodhounds of the capitalist gathering to decide our fate?
>
> Rise! Rise! Rise! . . .

Remember the place: Shanghai was its source, the one spot where the changes of China's Industrial Revolution were most advanced, and where the influence of Russia's Revolution was at that time strong. Remember the occasion: in its beginnings the Movement could not have been predominantly nationalist, or the target for its attack would hardly have been the Y.M.C.A., the first Christian organization in China to attain to Chinese control. Its nucleus seems to have been a student minority, in an exceptional environment, applying extremist theories from abroad. Perhaps such extremist and unrepresentative beginnings account for

From John Foster, *Chinese Realities* (London: Edinburgh House Press, 1928), pp. 135-40, 142-45, 147-54. Reprinted by permission of the publisher.

the fact that the Anti-Christians made little stir until towards the end of 1924. Then the Movement began to spread to other places, newspapers in various centres were led to publish anti-Christian supplements, and propaganda was widely issued in preparation for Christmas week, the time fixed for demonstrations against Christianity on something like a national scale. The secret of its widening influence is contained in these later declarations: both ground of appeal and ground of attack had widened. No longer is the point of view limited to that of Shanghai students engrossed in labour problems, no longer are the prevailing features so reminiscent of an importation from Russia. The features correspond more closely to the background of change throughout the whole of China, and the tone, happily, is more convincing of the presence of honest doubters among China's own youth.

Here is a declaration upon this broader basis. . . .

We oppose Religion because:

We are progressive, religion is conservative; it forbids doubt of ancient custom and creed.

We make for union, religion for disunion: witness the Crusades and the Thirty Years' War.

We follow science, religion follows superstition: in a college at Shanghai anti-evolutionist views are held by students.

We seek self-realization, religion seeks self-abasement: prayer and repentance make man dependent. . . .

We oppose Christian education because it is:

Despotic, there is no freedom of thought and action.

Superstitious, children are threatened with the devil.

Compulsory, non-Christians are forced to worship and to study the Bible.

Tyrannical, non-attendance at Sunday service results in stoppage of leave or going without a meal.

Conservative, text-books, matter, methods and discipline are old-fashioned. . . .

If it is true to say that the factors leading to the organization of the Anti-Christian Movement were the signs of Christianity's strength, it is equally true that its success was assured by young China's characteristic weaknesses: severance from the historic past, lack of adjustment to new and larger relationships, absence of any determined philosophy of life —the weakness inevitable to life in a ruin.

But the weakness is not all with them: the truth is rather that the failings on the one hand too often match the infirmities on the other. I must confess that I have sometimes felt that, were I a young Chinese, I might to-day be an ardent anti-Christian. . . .

I sometimes wonder what I should do if it had befallen me, as it has befallen some of my friends, suddenly to awake to so many problems that seem to require a radical revolutionary solution. . . .

There are pressing problems of society: not of a submerged tenth, but of a submerged nine-tenths. In the old days men wondered, as they saw our medical pioneers, at the care of Christianity for maimed and helpless individuals. But now young China looks for the salvation of a society that is maimed and helpless too. If I were a young Chinese, I might be intolerant of our village preacher, as behind the times and out of touch with modern needs. If so, I might listen to those who say that he is subsidized by money that comes—I know not how—from a "capitalist" country. I might even be ready to suspect—if I did not know his miserable pittance—that so long as he himself was raised above the struggle for a living wage, he would go on "saving souls."

Souls! Yes I too should be engrossed in bodies and houses and wages and welfare, more intent on theories which change a social system, than on a religion which says to individual men, Repent! Four hundred millions, one by one! Can youth wait for that, even if he believed that it would work? But these others talk of quicker and (supposedly) more radical measures, measures which leave no room for "the patient suffering of unnecessary evils," or a heaven where all will be put right.

Repentance, sin, the frailty of human nature, these were unwelcome doctrines in the old days, foreign to the philosophy of China, which, in the words of the school-book, declared that "Men one and all from infancy are virtuous at heart." But what now, in days when youth is hopeful of its future, trustful of its leaders, confident of building a new heaven and a new earth by the dispelling of ignorance, not sin, and the teaching of new principles, not a change of heart? Some even of our Chinese theological students are inclined to doubt the preaching of repentance, to neglect Christianity's central theme, redemption, to suspect emphasis upon the weakness of human nature (of which in recent history there is such abundant proof) as "casting reproach upon China." . . .

If I were a young Chinese, where should I stand? . . .

A few days ago, my own cook, a youth who has been in the employ of missionaries for nearly ten years, asked me if it was the British government that paid my salary! Why? Because disinterested service is hard for non-Christians to understand; because the patriotism of the foreigner is looked upon as his outstanding characteristic; because under the system of extra-territoriality, the necessary connection of a British citizen with his Consul may easily be misinterpreted in a land where connection with government has been for officials only. But if a man with such close and constant experience of us can misunderstand, what of the masses, whose only knowledge is the propaganda which they hear and the pictures which are shown to them?

Here is one such picture: it shows the foreigners entering through the hole they have battered in old China's wall. First comes the missionary bearing the Bible and the Cross. A mask covers his face, but his ears stick out—wolfish, devilish ears. Behind follow a cannon, a gunboat, and evil, smirking "imperialists." Surely, says the youth, it cannot be as bad as that! But stay—here are articles from newspapers and magazines with talk of "political aggression," and they prove that Christian missions have all along been its tool: "Britain, France and Germany compelled China to cede territory in compensation for the murder of missionaries. Eight nations together forced China to pay the huge Boxer Indemnity owing to trouble caused by Christianity." They almost imply that the deliberate intention of foreign Christians was to provide an opportunity for "imperialism" by being murdered! In the first flush of patriotism, youth forgets that it takes two to make a quarrel—or even a homicide—and the case against Christianity looks blacker than any murderer's.

Nor is that all. Writers bring abundant proof that missionaries who, as foreign citizens, share inevitably in the "unequal treaties," have often used their prestige as foreigners, or the security of their property as extra-territorial, to befriend their Chinese colleagues and members of the church. It may be that interest in a law-suit was an attempt to get a little justice from a corrupt court (though, of course, the writers do not say so); that the provision of "sanctuary" in the mission compound was from the looting, raping soldiery (though the articles, of course, omit to mention this also). But, whatever the occasion, in these days of nationalism who is a foreigner to interfere?

The young Chinese may never have heard of the persecution under Diocletian, or of the Roman fear of *imperium in imperio,* but, as he reads, it is some such danger to the nation that young nationalist China fears. He stays to ask no more, but dashes off to join the procession which even now is shouting in the street, as it marches to obstruct a Christian service at the church. He may be stirred sufficiently to break up a piece or two of church furniture, and a few windows as well—perhaps even to the extent of breaking a few heads, if need be. And "Down with the Imperialists!" he cries. Poor misguided young China. . . .

"Political aggression," "economic aggression," and thirdly, "cultural aggression"; that last is added to the original list as the name for all this preparatory infiltration of Christianity which is to make China subservient to the foreigner's will. They are vague and clumsy words, but here again are placards which explain. One shows young China seated in a chair. A missionary from behind has blindfolded him: and the words on the bandage are "Holy Bible."

If that is not enough, further explanations will not fail you, for this is now the leading phalanx of the anti-Christian attack. There is a good deal of jealousy of Christian schools, and jealousy and suspicion are related not only in dictionaries but in life. The budgets of Christian schools cannot be upset by appropriation of the funds; their discipline is less disturbed by the lawlessness of the student body; they stand out from the prevailing ruin, and, like everything outstanding, they are watched. Thus it becomes known that, while there is instruction in civics, no party propaganda is allowed; while there are students' societies, they are none of them political; while they keep "Double Ten" and a few other days, they do not have a holiday every time there is a demonstration. And yet Bible teaching is prominent in the curriculum; morning prayers and Sunday services are compulsory; they celebrate all the Christian, if not all the national, feasts. Foreign religion, instead of Chinese nationalism! "Christian schools denationalize."

Moreover, if their discipline is harder to upset, it is also harder, in these days of liberty and licence, to endure. There are malcontents within, and defaulters who have been put out. These have an eager audience when they prove conclusively (in public meeting or in newspapers, for there is no law of libel) that those secure funds are from "capitalist" sources, that this enforced discipline is a miniature "imperialism." "Every student who enters a mission school is one good soldier lost to the Revolution." And lo! these youths are defaulters and malcontents no more: in the twinkling of an eye they have been changed into patriots and martyrs. They even regard themselves as such, for China is somehow to be saved by "movements"—movements of arms and flags, and of fists that beat the air. "Down with the imperialism of the Christian schools!" Some indeed love the darkness better than the light; but, blind leaders of the blind, they are more to be pitied than blamed.

"Cultural aggression" has been the loudest war-cry, and Christian schools and colleges the chief objective, of recent anti-Christian attacks. The strategy employed is well summarized in the following plan of campaign. It was published by the National Federation of Student Unions in preparation for the winter of 1925-6:

The week about Christmas is to be anti-Christian week. In the winter holidays local student unions should send students to cities and villages, publishing the evils of Christianity. To aid this, handbills should be used. Special point should be made of the backwardness of Christianity, the plot of cultural aggression, stirring up students of mission schools to agitate for improvement in school affairs. Some members should themselves participate in Y.M.C.A. and other Church work, in order to agitate for bringing expenditure and work more into the open, and to oppose the small group of functionaries who keep everything in their own hands. . . .

The student unions should have some specially selected members to assist Christians to disentangle themselves from the toils of Christianity. Whenever and wherever we hear of Christians so doing, we should publish their names and the reason for their secession in all the newspapers, to show that these have been aroused, and so help other infatuated Christians to see the darkness of Christianity.

Later plans of the movement are said, by a Chinese writer, to be:

To establish its organziation in factories, young people's societies, even in mission schools and in the Church itself; to continue agitation for getting back [sic] control of education (i.e., by government); to get students leaving mission schools admitted into government schools unconditionally; to continue to give care to agitation which will lead Christians to denounce Christianity; to investigate the weak points of the Church.

These last two years they have advanced, at some points in the line, far beyond their objective. In many places soldiers, by occupying Christion schools and churches, have found an opportunity of striking an easy blow against "imperialism"—and, incidentally, of getting easy billets for themselves. In others labour unions have wrecked or closed schools, plastering them with placards. In many towns riots have taken place; in some, Christians have been led about the streets with placards on their backs. Some bear on their body the marks, the stigmata, of the Lord Jesus; and a few have followed Him to prison and to death. . . .

And now it is over: at any rate, it seems as if the worst is over.

From the start it was obvious that much in the anti-Christian Movement belonged to a temporary phase, part of the whirlwind of a destructive storm that must blow itself out in the end. It is the fashion these last few months in China to put down all excesses and extremes to the credit of departed Russians and executed Chinese communists. We need not wholeheartedly follow the fashion, but two facts are worthy of note. First, that since the fall of the Communist party from power, less and less has been heard of anti-Christian agitation. And second, that such agitation plainly has no basis in "orthodox" nationalism. The only significant reference to Christianity in *The Three People's Principles* is surely significant enough. After comparing the teaching of the philosopher Mo Tzu about love with that of Jesus, Sun Yat Sen continues:

> With the increasing intercourse between Chinese and foreigners, some have come to think that the love Chinese have talked of is surpassed by the foreigners. For they have set up schools and opened hospitals in China, to teach and to save Chinese. This belongs to love's *expression*. . . . Chinese, with regard to love, have not yet equalled foreigners in this kind of expression.

However else we are misrepresented and misunderstood, it seems that Sun Yat Sen did not misunderstand us here.

20 / CHRISTIANITY, THE CHAMPION OF NATIONALISM

Wherever in Asia and Africa the ruling imperial power was nominally Christian, the nationalist thrust tended to be opposed to Christianity. But where, as in Korea, the ruling power was non-Christian, Christianity emerged as a focus and champion of the national movement. Korean Christianity has been one of the most vital expressions of the Christian faith in Asia, closely linked to the national leadership of the country throughout this century. When in the 1930s Japan embarked on a program of expansion in East Asia, the militarist leaders of the program believed that it was necessary to unite the people of Korea as well as of Japan in support of their great undertaking. To that end they initiated a revival and extension of the Shinto faith in Korea and thus came into open conflict with the Christian Church. It will be clear from what follows that the Christians were trying to be true to the demands of their faith rather than presenting themselves as the champions of nationalism, but that championship followed inevitably.

The Shinto Shrine Controversy in Korea

In the fall of 1935, the Japanese governor of South Pyengan Province invited Dr. George S. McCune, president of the Union Christian College, and Miss V. L. Snook, principal of the Soongeui Girls' High School,

From Allen D. Clark, *History of the Korean Church* (Seoul: Christian Literature Society of Korea, n.d.) pp. 194-97, 200-201. Reprinted by permission of the publisher.

in Pyengyang, to attend a conference of educational leaders of the province in his office. At the opening of the conference, the governor rose and said, "Today, before we take up the agenda, we will all go by car to the new Shinto Shrine and pay respects." The word used was a word meaning "worship." This placed the two representatives of the Christian schools in a very difficult position.

"Your honor," said Dr. McCune, "Miss Snook and I must ask you to excuse us from going, because it is impossible for us, as Christians, to take part in such ceremonies." The governor probably expected such a reply, but answered, "Why can't you go? You must go, or it will be considered an insult to the Emperor." They tried to explain, but the governor ordered them to go home and consider the matter for 60 days, at the end of which time, if they did not change their attitude, their educational qualifications would be taken away.

They informed the missionaries in Pyengyang and the Mission Executive Committee of what had happened. They then called a meeting of the Korean pastors of the 27 Presbyterian churches in the city. All but one strongly advised them to refuse to go to the shrines, no matter what happened. The outstanding leader of the group ended by saying, "You have heard what has been said. We know that the worship of deified spirits at the shrines is contrary to God's commandments. We also know that terrible pressure will be put on the Korean Church, that many of us will not be able to withstand. Therefore, we ask you missionaries today, while we are able to speak, to protect the faith of the Church, no matter what happens."

The missionaries in Pyengyang felt that this settled the matter. They accepted the judgment of their Korean brethren, freely and clearly given that day, as a solemn and sacred trust. Under later pressure, many Korean leaders weakened and apparently changed their attitude, but there is no reason to doubt the sincerity and rightness of the position taken in that memorable conference.

A highly educated Korean friend who had studied in Japan said, "For fifty years, the Mission and the Korean Church have taught that worship of any spirit other than God is wrong. Shinto is not only ancestor worship, but worship of deified ancestors. If we now, under pressure, in order to save our schools, give in and take part in Shinto ceremonies, nobody will believe that we are sincere. We will have no power to preach the Gospel."

At the end of 60 days, a letter was sent to the governor thanking him for past favors and explaining why it was impossible to bow at the

Shrine. The governor had apparently already decided what to do. Both Dr. McCune and Miss Snook were notified that their educational qualifications were revoked. Police were sent to "guard" Dr. McCune's door and examined and abused all Koreans who came near the house. He was followed by the police wherever he went and was practically driven from the country within three months.

At this point, an effort was made to come to an understanding with the Educational Department of the Government-General. Mr. Oda, a representative of the Foreign Office in Seoul and a professing Christian, came to Pyengyang and asked why they could not attend the shrines as a patriotic act, which was all the government required. He was asked "Are there, or are there not, spirits other than God worshiped in these government-required ceremonies? If the government will officially declare that the ceremonies are only patriotic and that there are no spirits being worshiped there or supposed to be worshiped there, this will relieve our consciences greatly." "No," he said, "I am afraid that is impossible, because the great majority of the Japanese people believe that spirits are being worshiped in these ceremonies."

Meanwhile, efforts were being made to find a means of satisfying the government's desire to foster patriotism without violating Christian principles. In some places, it was permitted to bow to the flag, or to bow [to] the picture of the Emperor, or to carry on some patriotic ceremony on the school grounds. But these were never allowed to become a precedent. Before long, something else would be required. There must be a bow toward the East, toward the Emperor's palace in Tokyo. Then the school was ordered to bow toward the East, toward the Yse Shrine in Tokyo. Then the school was ordered to attend a ceremony at the Shrine, but standing on a lower terrace than the terrace of the main Shrine itself. Then they were ordered to stand in front of the actual Shrine. Step by step, the pressure was exerted. Every effort was made to persuade some weak Christian, in one place, to do what was demanded. Then, when someone else in another place demurred, he was told that So-and-so had done so and he is a Christian, then why can't you? Pressure was brought on Christian parents by expelling their children from school, if they were not permitted to take part in these ceremonies. . . .

Some schools were closed rather than discuss the principles involved. Some were continued until continuing seemed impossible. Some were transferred to other bodies which found it possible to carry on without conscientious scruples. It was a confused time.

Pressures on the church governing bodies became steadily stronger and stronger. Finally, a committee of Japanese church leaders was brought over to Korea to tour the country, urging Korean church leaders to accept the government's interpretation, as they had done in Japan. This proved a very strong argument, for many.

Finally, two weeks before the Presbyterian General Assembly was to meet in Pyengyang, in 1938, the Chief of Police called in the missionaries and told them that the Assembly would be required to pass an action approving Shrine worship and ordering them not to interfere. They were told that there would be no debate permitted and that no one would be permitted to vote against it, as that would be an insult to the Emperor.

All the 100 delegates to the Assembly were summoned to their local police offices in advance and told that they must vote for the motion, when presented on the first day of the Assembly. They all tried to present excuses for not being able to attend the Assembly, but the police told them that they must go to Pyengyang and vote as directed or go to prison. Many of them went to prison. Nearly all who went to Pyengyang were accompanied by police escort. The day before the Assembly opened, all the missionary delegates were called to the office of the Pyengyang Chief of Police who read them a statement of what would be done, the next day, and ordering them to say nothing in the meeting. The next day, at the time agreed upon, a delegate rose and moved as he had been ordered to do, another seconded the motion and a third spoke for the motion, all according to orders. The moderator, in accordance with police instructions, began to put the question. Rev. W. N. Blair had been named by the missionary group to speak against this. He rose to his feet and bedlam broke loose, with the police shouting and running forward to stop him. When there was a lull in the noise, he asked the moderator's permission to speak, but this was denied, whereupon he said, "Then I demand that my name be enrolled on the minutes as protesting this action as contrary to the laws of God and of our Church." Eight or ten other missionaries made the same demand. The moderator then put the question, and there were only a few "Yeas." The motion was passed without putting the negative, which was, of course, an illegal proceeding.

With this tool in their hands, the police then went on to break all resistance throughout the Church.

21 / CHRISTIANITY AS A TOOL OF NATIONALISM

The pressures of nationalism have at times produced not a conflict but a complete accommodation on the part of Christians. This is a phenomenon more familiar in the West than in the non-Western parts of the world: self-styled Christian movements of an extremely nationalistic nature have appeared often in Europe and America. In the Orient one of the clearest examples of this accommodation occurred in Japan during the Second World War. The government at that time made demands for extreme forms of nationalist expression on the part of Christians and imposed them rigorously. Some Christians refused to cooperate and suffered imprisonment and death, but the major Christian bodies did as they were told. An American who was in Japan immediately after the war gathered information on what had happened, and the following examples are taken from his report.

Accommodation in Wartime Japan

[A] striking identification of Christianity with the prevailing Shinto ideology is seen in the following statement from Akira Ebisawa, executive secretary of the highest Protestant council in Japan:

> What is then the plan for the long-term reconstruction of East Asia? Its purpose is that of realizing the vision emblazoned on the banner, "The world one family"; and that purpose, we must recognize afresh, coincides spontaneously with the fundamental faith of Christianity. The policy of extending even to the continent our family principle, which finds its center in an imperial house, so that all may bathe in its holy benevolence, this policy—can we not see?—is none other than the concrete realization on earth of the spiritual family principle of Christianity, which looks up to God as the Father of mankind and regards all men as brethren. This is the Christian conception of the Kingdom of God. The basis of the Japanese spirit also consists in this; and thus, wonderful to relate, it is one with Christianity. Nay, this must indeed be the Great Way of heaven and earth. . . .
>
> Herein is the reason why we, in this emergency, must make it our supreme and immediate duty to serve the country by preaching the gospel of Christ. To store up spiritual strength to regulate the various dislocations that the

From Richard Terrill Baker, *Darkness of the Sun. The Story of Christianity in the Japanese Empire* (New York and Nashville: Abingdon Press, 1947), pp. 30-31, 33. Reprinted by permission of the publisher.

"incident" produces within the nation itself; to help the people to make that progress in both physique and character which will fit them for the fulfillment of their mission; to enable them to burn with the ideal of the establishment of a new East Asia; and to stand firm in the assurance that it will be accomplished; thus to make us as a nation, face to face as we are with unprecedented difficulties, ready to sacrifice gladly for the development of the life of the ancestral country. . . . This, we believe, can be the work only of those who share the faith and life of Christianity.

On numerous occasions the United Church of Christ in Japan was guilty of handing down direct governmental orders to its local churches. One of these cases had to do with the officially prescribed five-minute ceremony of bowing to the emperor and praying for the war heroes just preceding every Christian service of worship. It was a compulsory ritual, and if for any reason it was ever neglected the pastor was immediately taken by the police for questioning.

In most Christian services the five-minute ritual was awkward and somewhat offensive. Many church-goers purposely tried to be from three to five minutes late to avoid it. Sometimes the ceremony was observed in the churchyard outside the sanctuary; sometimes it was a five-minute preliminary ritual inside the church, with the call to worship and musical prelude following. Sometimes it was part of the worship itself. Most of my informants on the subject of this little ritual agreed that it looked like a Shinto desecration of the house of God, but actually in the way it was handled by individual pastors it was not unchristian. The bow was a tribute to the national community, the prayer was a facing of God in silence and for whatever heartfelt petitions the worshiper wished to place before him. In postwar Japan no churches observe it. . . .

On December 28, 1942, the *Nippon Times* carried the following item, indicative of the part the church was playing in Japan's imperialistic plans:

Catholics in the Philippines are collaborating freely and willingly in the reconstruction of their motherland, it was revealed here recently in a letter from Bishop Yoshigoro Taguchi, who is now in Manila entrusted with the task of aiding spiritual guidance to the Filipinos, states Domei. . . . Bishop Taguchi's conviction that the Catholics in the Philippines are supporting earnestly and freely the Japanese military administration was reaffirmed when he addressed on November 14 a group of Filipino public officers who were then enrolled in a school established for retraining them in the discharge of their duties.

When the Philippines were "freed" and their independent government launched, Catholics in both Japan and the Philippines celebrated with services and public orations marking the event. In the October 15, 1943, issue of the *Nippon Times* appeared an article describing a service held in Tokyo, with the Rev. Shoji Tsukamoto taking part to celebrate the independence [i.e., the Japanese control] of the Philippines. Father Tsukamoto had been one of the Japanese religious mission to the Philippines.

22 / CHRISTIANITY, THE FOUNDATION OF NATIONALISM

Nationalism has become one of the principal subjects of non-Western Christian thought. Sometimes the thought has been negative, pointing out the idolatrous tendencies of faith in the nation or the unethical elements in the tactics of the nationalists. More often the approach has been positive, stressing the ways in which nationalism fits in with Christian beliefs, or even is derived from them. The official Church statements which have come out of Asia and Africa in recent years have been primarily of the latter type, though the attitudes of ordinary pastors and priests have often been of the former.

In Africa most of the nationalist leaders have been at least nominally, and sometimes seriously, committed to Christian faith. Those closely related to the Church have devoted considerable thought to the implications of Christianity for African nationalism. An example of the interest in the Christian sources of nationalism is to be found in the writings of Ndabaningi Sithole, who is both a Christian minister and a nationalist leader in Rhodesia. Sithole long worked with Joshua Nkomo, the principal African political figure of Rhodesia, in the leadership of the Zimbabwe African Peoples' Union. More recently he has broken with Nkomo and leads the rival Zimbabwe African National Union.

An African Christian View

What is the actual relevance of the Bible or the New Testament to African nationalism? We need not elaborate to any great length that the Bible has most powerful ideas for the heart and for the mind. No man can be brought up on the Bible and remain uninfluenced by it. If it is true that the teachings of the Holy Bible greatly helped in the shaping

From Ndabaningi Sithole, *African Nationalism* (Cape Town: Oxford University Press, 1959), pp. 55-57. Reprinted by permission of the publisher.

of European thought, the same thing could be said of Africa. If it is true that the United States owes much to the Bible, the same thing could be said of Africa.

One of the unique teachings of the Bible, especially the New Testament, is the worth and dignity of the individual in the sight of God, and there is a relation between this teaching and the present African nationalism. According to African tradition, at least in some parts if not in the whole of Africa, the individual counted in so far as he was part and parcel of the group, outside of which he lost his real worth. . . . But now the African individual is being delivered from these fetters. The individual is being invested with a new status, and so today we find individuals venturing beyond the confines of the group, and in many cases the group now looks upon this new individual as its real saviour. The Bible is redeeming the African individual from the power of superstition, individuality-crushing tradition, witchcraft, and other forces that do not make for progress. The same Bible is helping the African individual to reassert himself above colonial powers! It is inconceivable to a logical mind that the Bible could deliver the African from traditional domination without at the same time redeeming him from colonial domination. If the Bible teaches that the individual is unique, of infinite worth before God, colonialism, in many respects, says just the opposite; so that, in actual practice, Biblical teachings are at variance with colonialism, and it becomes only a matter of time before one ousts the other. The Bible-liberated African is now reasserting himself not only over tribal but also over colonial authority, since these two are fundamentally the same. . . .

But it is not only the African Christian who stands against those forces which deny him freedom. True European Christians are also on the side of the African, but perhaps this is to state the matter rather incorrectly since there is no particular virtue in being on the side of either the African or the European. It is more correct to say that true European Christians are standing on the side of that which is right— namely, that oppression or suppression of any human being is wrong. What goes on in colonial Africa shocks the Christian conscience of both black and white so that, in a real sense, white supremacy finds itself engaged in a life-and-death struggle with Christian principles. The Anglican Church of South Africa, for instance, has taken an uncompromising position on the apartheid policy. When the Nationalist Government of the Union of South Africa introduced the new Native Laws

Amendment Bill (1957) which would bar interracial gatherings of any kind, the late Archbishop Clayton, in collaboration with four other Anglican bishops, wrote to the Prime Minister and stressed the official position of the Anglican Church, which is the second largest denomination in the country:

> The Church cannot recognize the right of an official of the secular Government to determine whether or where a member of the Church of any race (who is not serving a sentence which restricts his freedom of movement) shall discharge his religious duty in participation in public worship, or to give instructions to the minister of any congregation as to whom he shall admit to membership of the congregation. . . .

It is not only the Anglican Church that is battling against racial discrimination, but also such denominations as the Methodist, Roman Catholic, Congregational, and Salvation Army. This is not only true of South Africa, but of such countries as the Federation of Rhodesia and Nyasaland, British East Africa, and other African countries where Christian churches and Christian councils fight for ordinary human justice for the African.

We have had to quote at length in order to show that the Christian Church has created in Africa, at least in some parts of Africa, a strong Christian consciousness that transcends the usual barriers of race and colour, and this Christian consciousness is based on the love of God and the love of our fellow-men. It is based on a strong sense of human justice. The story of African nationalism would be incomplete if this Christian awareness was ignored since it is this awareness that is an integral part of the creativeness of African nationalism. . . .

Of course, the non-Christians also support this movement. But while African nationalism is strongly motivated by African consciousness of an oppressed people seeking freedom, it is Christian consciousness that gives it the proper direction and that self-sustaining creativity which makes for human progress. The Christian faith may be regarded in one sense as its spiritual father, whether or not the Church recognizes that role. In another sense, the Church may be regarded as the guardian angel of African nationalism. Practically all important African political leaders went through the Christian Church school. The African politician may turn his nose up in derision, and twist his lips by way of deprecation, when he hears it said that the Christian Church laid secure political foundations for African nationalism, but that need not surprise us, for two reasons. First,

> But 'tis a common proof,
> That lowliness is young ambition's ladder,
> Whereto the climber-upward turns his face;
> But when he once attains the upmost round,
> He then unto the ladder turns his back,
> Looks in the clouds, scorning the base degrees
> By which he did ascend.

And second, a few missionaries, working in a colonial atmosphere, also adopted a colonial attitude towards the African and stood between the latter and his big dream of independence. The few erring missionaries, however, should not be confused with the main stream of missionaries who, by example and precept, have demonstrated the reality of Christian principles. The fact is that the Christian faith is like a highly prolific fruit tree whose fruit gives life to those who care and to those who do not care for it. Christian and non-Christian Africans have reaped, in varying degrees, the blessings of the Christian faith, and this is as it should be since God himself sends rain on the just and the unjust.

THE CONFRONTATION WITH COMMUNISM

23 / RESISTANCE TO COMMUNISM

Christianity has encountered Communism in many parts of the non-Western world. The Indian state of Kerala, which is the one place in the world where Communism has come to power through free elections and where it happens that a large percentage of the population is Christian, has been the scene of a vigorous Communist-Christian debate. Vietnam and Korea have shown some of the varieties of Communist repression of Christianity. But the principal theater of the encounter has been China. There the Christians have gone through many stages of contact with Communists, revealing much about both groups.

Inevitably, the contacts involved both resistance and cooperation. Resistance in some form could not be avoided, because the Communists made no secret of the fact that they were dedicated to the eventual disappearance of all religions, including Christianity. Cooperation at certain points, however, was equally unavoidable if Christianity was to carry on the business of living in a society ruled by Communism.

The following selections give examples of both resistance and cooperation. It will be noted that neither of these took place in terms of the Communist opposition to religion or the Christian concern for human existence, which are the deeper issues involved, but occurred on a com-

paratively superficial and peripheral issue, that of the Western contacts —the "imperialist connections"—of Christianity. Here was the point of Communist attack, and here the Christians were drawn both to resistance insofar as they believed in unity with all of the body of Christ and to co-operation insofar as they believed that Chinese Christianity should not become merely a dependency of some other form of Christianity. Those who stressed the latter belief led in the movement to reform the Church in accordance with the government's wishes—the Movement of the Three Autonomies, or the Three-Self Reform Movement, as it was called (self-government, self-support, and self-propagation being the three "selfs" referred to). Those who resisted such reform did so partly because they wanted to maintain unity with Christians abroad and partly because they suspected this reform as being the first stage of a total attack on the Church.

The Experience of a Parish

Nanning is an example of the fate of a small Christian community in a big city; here the persecution took many different forms during its development, and the resistance of the Christians was magnificent throughout.

Nanning, which is in the province of Kwangsi, has a population of 180,000, which includes barely 400 Catholics in the city itself; it also has a seminary with five Chinese priests as teachers and twenty students, a convent with forty nuns or novices, a Catholic school with a hundred pupils, and a much frequented dispensary for the sick.

By September 1950 the newspapers had been discussing the "Reform" of the Protestant "patriots" for several months. Various Protestant sects had disavowed the "imperialism" which was supposed to be represented by the Pope, the Catholic Church and the foreign missionaries and in several places the Catholics were approached and asked to follow their example.

But the Communist campaign was not yet properly under way, since its agents, for lack of direct instructions, were not yet sure of the best method of attack, and were simply exploring the ground. At the end of 1950 the "Registration" of the different works, personnel, and goods of the Catholic Mission furnished them with abundant information, which there was little doubt that they intended to use against the Church. The alarm sounded when they demanded certain things, like a list of

From Jean Monsterleet, *Martyrs in China,* translated by Antonia Pakenham (Chicago: Henry Regnery Co., 1956), pp. 109-11, 115-19. Reprinted by permission of the author and Longmans, Green & Co. Ltd.

all the Christians in the city: however, in spite of repeated requests and threats, the list was not handed over, and in consequence relations became increasingly strained.

In the New Year two Communists, Comrades Fan and Lung, were dispatched from the Liaison Centre of all the Communist movements, entrusted with the task of promoting the "Reform." Their first action was to seek out the Chinese priests and certain influential Chinese laymen whom they had marked down—for example a lay teacher at the seminary, the president of the Legion of Mary, a lecturer, and the Librarian—and ask them to sign a manifesto in favour of the "Reform" as a proof of their patriotism. . . .

The Christians were taken by surprise by this attack and took counsel among themselves. They decided to answer the Communists' demands with a categorical refusal, and individual Christians were warned not to sign the manifesto for the "Three Autonomies" if it was presented to them. The following Sunday the parish priest brought things to a head by announcing from the pulpit that the "Reform" which was hostile to the hierarchy, was also against the laws of the Church. He threatened with excommunication those who acted in any way against the ecclesiastical authorities.

At the beginning of 1951 the Protestants in Nanning signed a manifesto in favour of the Reform: it had been put before them as a purely patriotic movement which had nothing to do with faith. The Catholics were told that they were the only ones who had refused to perform this patriotic gesture, and that by so doing, they were branding themselves as imperialist foreigners. Some of the Catholics were taken in by this and persuaded themselves that they were strengthening the position of the Church by signing the manifesto and performing an act of patriotism.

At that time it was still possible to hold this view in good faith, for the impossibility of relations between the Catholics and the Communists was not yet realized. On 1 February, in order to put pressure upon the waverers, Father Joseph Mung, parish priest of the Wumin district, 30 miles from Nanning, was arrested on a charge of being an imperialist agent. After refusing to lead the Reformed Church in Nanning, he was imprisoned, to be condemned a year later to ten years' penal servitude. Every day the Christians could see the mass of convicts in red trousers and guess the fate which was in store for them, and at length, after consultation with the bishop, a demonstration was in fact organized against America, although all mention of the Reform was excluded from it. Even so, at the actual meeting the mass of Christians showed themselves hostile to the whole under taking. . . .

During all this time the underground movement was going forward. A Communist went round the Christian families who had lapsed and made them sign a declaration in favour of the "Reform" on the pretext that it was an unimportant formality. But he made the mistake of soliciting several practising Christians at the same time and these noticed in his book about sixty signatures, among them the names of several practising Christians who had been tricked into signing. The next day about ten of them signed a retraction, in which they dissociated themselves from the "Reform" and the signature which had been wrongfully won from them. Thenceforth all the Catholics were on their guard, and the signatures which had been already obtained proved useless. Once more the "Reform" which had been planned for the first of May misfired.

After the first of May the Christians continued to be summoned to the Town Hall in groups, where the talk always centred round the subject of the "Reform." The Christian Communist brought his conquests there—a few apostates or lapsed Catholics who called themselves Chinese patriots and pretended that they were leading a widespread movement.

The administration was determined to score a triumph, and announced that there would be an "assembly for accusations." The Christians were warned, and about 200 of them turned up; there were some "reformists" there, and about a dozen Communists sent by the Liaison Centre to direct the whole operation. At eight o'clock at night the assembly was opened by a menacing speech from a Communist from the Liaison Centre. Then the principal Catholic delegate, M. Ts'uo, mounted the platform and succeeded in speaking for ten minutes, in spite of the efforts of the Communists to stop him, about the Eighth Commandment, the necessity of honouring the truth and respecting the reputation of others. The Christians, whom the Communists had tried to divide up into little groups, applauded him loudly; after that they did make accusations for four hours, but they spoke entirely about crimes committed by the Japanese during the war, and the good work which the Catholic Mission had done during the occupation. They were jubilant, and the three priests present felt proud of their flock. Rightly so—for although other assemblies had been announced, they never took place. It was the first great victory of the Nanning Catholics. . . .

In face of this set-back, the Communists laboriously returned to the attack at Nanning with political study circles of about thirty people at the Mission—school teachers, catechists, nuns, novices, and members of the Mission. June and July passed like this, with the Christians protesting and leaving whenever the question of "Reform" was raised. Several speakers were replaced no doubt for lack of skill. At all times the constant pressure to sign some form of manifesto in favour of Reform was kept up.

The assault on the Catholics was continued not only within these study circles: wherever they were recognized as such, the battle went on —in the unions, in the meetings of the local administration even. At the end of July two teachers who were taking part in a course of political training were summoned to sign the manifesto for the "Three Autonomies." They refused point-blank, after which they were left in peace. . . .

One Sunday evening, just before Mass, the news of Father Bede Tsang's death reached Nanning, and the priest informed the parish of it in his sermon. Proudly and fearlessly, the whole congregation sang the "Song of Martyrs" to his memory, for the persecution of the missionaries only stimulated their courage. To the north-east of Nanning in April 1951 Father Martin Chiang, a priest of 64, who had always been distinguished by his zeal and his self-abnegation, was arrested on the pretext that he had given asylum to some "nationalist bandits," and had indulged in other activities contrary to the welfare of the people. He was shut up in his little church, which had been turned into a prison, and already contained more than a hundred prisoners. During his confinement, he was able to baptize about fifteen of his companions in misfortune. As he had to sleep on the bare and humid earth, in stifling heat, at the end of about three months he fell gravely ill; he was then released on bail, and allowed to look after himself in his tiny house. However, he died shortly after on 17 September 1951. At about the same time, in the neighbouring mission of Pakhoi, Father Liu died, after eight days of horrible torture. All this was known to the Christians —who knew also that their turn might come next, and held themselves in readiness from one day to the next.

24 / COOPERATION WITH COMMUNISM

Gradually those who favored cooperation gained the upper hand in the churches. The old structures of Church life were destroyed or superseded, and new structures created for the reforming purpose took their place. The National Christian Council, for example, simply disappeared, and its role was assumed by the China Christian Three-Self Patriotic Movement. This body tried to make a place for Christianity in the new society, but it did so at the expense of destroying much of the Christianity that existed. It examined all Christian books and had large quantities of those labeled "imperialist" burned by their publishers, even though there was little prospect of any further Christian publication to replace what was lost. It agreed that most Christian periodicals were unnecessary and arranged for their suspension. The most severe blow that it dealt to Christian life and Christian convictions was its sponsorship of the accusation movement. In this movement Christians were turned against each other and made to denounce each other as fiercely as any Communist would have denounced them. Accusation meetings were made a prerequisite for the establishment of local Three-Self Committees where they were not already in existence. Though in other times and other countries Christians have suffered greater repression and persecution from Communists, the accusation movement stands as the most agonizing experience that the Church has endured under Communism. The following instructions for accusation meetings were published in Shanghai in 1951. Ku Jen-en, referred to in the instructions, was a traveling evangelist singled out as a favorite target of Communist attacks. He was already in jail at the time, and was never again heard from. Frank Price was an American missionary, a secretary of the Church of Christ in China in Shanghai, far from imperialist in his sympathies but for some strange reason selected as a prime target.

How To Hold a Successful Accusation Meeting

One of the central tasks at present for Christian churches and groups across the nation is to hold successful accusation meetings.

Why do we want to accuse? Because for more than a hundred years

From *Documents of the Three Self Movement* (New York: Far Eastern Office, Division of Foreign Missions [now Asia Department, Division of Overseas Ministries], National Council of the Churches of Christ in the U.S.A. 1963), pp. 49-51. Reprinted by permission of the publisher.

imperialism has utilized Christianity to attack China, therefore we want to accuse it of its sins. As a result of the longtime influence of imperialism, many Christians have the old-fashioned idea of "being above politics"; therefore we must hold accusation meetings to educate everybody. Big accusation meetings constitute a most effective means of helping the masses of believers to comprehend the evils wrought in China by imperialism, to recognize the fact that imperialism has utilized Christianity to attack China, and to wipe out imperialist influences within the churches.

Accuse what? We must accuse imperialist elements and their helpers as well as other bad elements hidden in the churches. We want to expose their sin of utilizing the churches to attack China and deceive believers. For example, many Christians in Tsingtao, Shanghai, Hangchow and Peking have accused America's political agent, Ku Jen-en, of wearing the cloak of religion to engage in counter-revolutionary activities, and even rumor-mongering and swindling, raping women and killing sick people. Christian leaders such as Ts'ui Hsien-hsiang and Chiang Ch'ang-ch'uan have accused imperialist elements, Frank Price, etc., who take the name of missionary to carry on special agent activities, and other special agents of America and Chiang [Kai-shek] who hold high positions in the churches.

How shall we hold a successful accusation meeting? First, we must remove the thought barriers of many Christians. Some Christians suppose that they ought to "hide evil and display good" or that they ought not to accuse. And yet Jesus' reprimands to the Scribes and Pharisees of that time were certainly accusations. Some Christians feel that they are "unable to accuse of some things"; they ought then to participate more in the big accusation meetings of people from all walks of life and the public trials of counter-revolutionaries. The anger and charges of the masses of the people towards imperialism, bandits, and wicked tyrants will arouse the righteous indignation and accusations of Christians towards imperialism and bad elements in the churches.

Second, if we want to hold a successful accusation meeting, we must first do well the preparatory work. Every church and the city-wide church federation ought to first organize an accusation committee. They should first study whom they want to accuse, and whom to invite to do the accusing. After this they should invite those participating in the accusation to attend a meeting to mobilize accusations so that they may understand why, what and how they should accuse. The second step of the preparation work is to hold in every church and group preliminary accusation meetings. In these meetings we should urge everyone to enthusiastically express his opinions and accuse. In this way we shall be able to discover a few people who accuse with the greatest power and invite them to participate in the large accusation meeting and can also correct weaknesses in their speaking, for example, making briefer the speeches which are too long, making clearer the speeches which are unclear, and making fuller the content of those which are insufficient.

Third, what can be considered to be a successful accusation meeting? According to the experience of Ts'ui Hsien-Hsiang, who accused Frank Price, accusations (1) ought to be according to facts; (2) must break through all sentimentality; (3) must in every sentence be spoken from the depths of the heart; (4) must be thorough-going, outspoken, sincere and uninhibited; (5) must hold firmly to the position of the people. Bishop Chiang Ch'ang-ch'uan of the Methodist Church, when he accused that bad element of the church, Ch'en Wen-yuan [another Methodist bishop], said "I am determined to purge my church in the spirit of unmitigated punishment of offenders, no matter who they are, definitely cleaning out thoroughly all elements like Ch'en Wen-yuan; if there is one, remove one, if there are ten, remove ten!" This sort of accusation moves people very deeply.

Fourth, the atmosphere of the meeting must be dignified when carrying on a local church or city-wide accusation meeting. The order of arrangement of the accusers is very important; they should be arranged as follows: first high tension, then moderate, then another of high tension, etc.; only so can the accusation meeting be a success. When the accusations have succeeded in deeply stirring people, clapping and applause may be used as a form of expression. Throughout the whole process of preparation for the big accusation meeting, we ought to invite the Religious Affairs Bureau of the local People's Government or other related offices, democratic political groups and other concerned parties to come and advise. The texts of outstanding accusations ought to be recorded and given to local papers for publishing, and also mailed to the Preparation Committee of the Chinese Christian Oppose-America Assist-Korea Three-Self Reform Movement Committee (address: 131 Museum Road, Shanghai). If there is evidence of specific crimes of imperialist elements or bad elements in the churches, such as correspondence, pictures, weapons, radios, etc., these must be reported to the local police office; and after obtaining the agreement of the police office, we may open a local exhibit of concrete materials, or mail them directly to the Preparation Committee of the Chinese Christian Oppose-America Assist-Korea Three-

Self Reform Movement Committee for use in a nationwide exhibition.

What about after the accusation? After the accusation the patriotic fervor and political comprehension of the masses of believers will be raised and they will have a much clearer understanding of imperialism. We ought to encourage the whole body of workers and fellow-believers in the church and all Christians to carry out the following tasks: (1) Strengthen study of current affairs; (2) Continue promoting the Three-Self Reform Movement; (3) Continue cleaning out all imperialist and bad elements within the churches; (4) Participate in local and national movements for the suppression of counter-revolution; (5) And actively participate in the Oppose-America Assist-Korea movement.

To hold a successful big accusation meeting is one of the important tasks that every church must do well to wipe out the influences of imperialism!

INDIGENOUS EXPRESSIONS OF CHRISTIANITY

25 / THE INDEPENDENT AFRICAN CHURCHES

The mid-twentieth century has witnessed the most rapid indigenization of Christianity in Africa. Roman Catholics and Protestants alike have laid new stress on the training of African clergy and have begun to reinterpret Christianity in African terms. The most radical reinterpretation of the faith and Africanization of forms has taken place, however, not in Roman Catholic or Protestant circles but in the independent movements initiated by African "prophets." In some cases the reinterpretation has been so sweeping as to raise doubts whether the result can still be called Christian. The kind of extreme indigenization which appeared in Asia in the nineteenth century with movements like the Taiping and the Brahmo Samaj has appeared in Africa in the twentieth.

In South Africa over two thousand independent church movements with over a million followers now exist. In areas further north the movements came later and are therefore fewer in number, yet in Nigeria, for example, some seventy-seven independent churches have been registered with the government. These movements usually began under the inspiration of a gifted leader—a "prophet"—who, after a powerful religious experience, broke away from one of the established churches. Studies of the movements often relate them to the social maladjustment and uncertainty which have characterized the impact of new culture on the old in Africa. At times these movements have expressed in religious forms a political opposition to foreign rule. They have also allowed for many of the more traditional African beliefs and practices under Christian nomenclature; polygamy is the most noticeable example. Many of them have stressed emotional experiences and faith healing.

For worldwide fame none of them has equaled the Lumpa Church of Zambia. This body is of recent origin, but it sprang to world attention when its followers fell into a misunderstanding with the newly independent government of their country and inaugurated a revolt in which they believed they would be invulnerable. They were suppressed by armed force, and their leader, Alice Lenshina, was persuaded to take a more cooperative attitude. The Lumpa Church, as described in the following extract, is closer than other sects to traditional Christianity because of its vigorous rejection of polygamy and of any use of protective magic.

The Lumpa Church

The beginning of the Lumpa Church is best described by the African minister who was from the start deeply involved, as he was in charge of the congregation in which the prophetess entered the catechumenate and was being prepared for church membership. He wrote a report to the Presbytery of the CCAR in April 1955:

In the district of Chinsali in the village of Kasomo in the country of chief Nkula a woman, Alice Mulenga Lenshina Lubusha, the wife of Petro Chintankwa, came back from the dead in September 1954. She came back to her senses from a faint in her illness. Then she called the Christian people, women of her village, that they should come and pray for her to God. When they had prayed she got up and went outside the village to sit under a tree. People wanted to go and watch her but she stopped them. When the sun set one woman went, because, she said, she may be posseessed by an *ngulu*. But Alice drove her away. "Go back to the village," she said, "I do not want anybody to watch me here." She wanted her husband and he went there but nobody else.

During that week many people heard that Lenshina Mulenga had come back from the dead. And angels had brought her books which came from heaven. And Jesus had come to speak to her. The people of Kasomo were very astonished to hear that Lenshina had died and come back from the dead; they did not know where this tale came from.

At that time Alice started to proclaim the Good News with all her power, and telling people many things about Jesus Christ. She said that the people should stop adultery and hatred and cursing and stealing and lies and swearing. She composed a new hymn: "A man who does not repent and believe in Jesus, he cannot stand near the judgment throne of God"; a song which is good in its words and its parable. . . .

From John V. Taylor, *Christians of the Copperbelt* (London: SCM Press Ltd., 1961), pp. 248-50, 252-56, 261-63, 265-66. Reprinted by permission of the publisher.

In December (the beginning of the planting season) she started to give people seeds to mix with their own seeds and blessings for their seeds. And unfortunately she started to baptize people. The minister and the elders tried to stop her but she refused. She started to tell people: "Bring your magic, horns and charms, then you will be saved in God's judgment." And those who were already baptized came to be baptized by her a second time, Protestants as well as Roman Catholics, very many people from the districts of Chinsali, Kasama, Abercorn, Isoka, Lundazi and Mpika. Old and young, some made a journey of 150 miles, coming and going. Everybody had to give a penny, and the mother gave a penny to the baby on her back to throw into the gift basket.

At night Lenshina played an instrument [a reed pipe?], and said: "Come, hear what God is telling you," and she herself interpreted what it meant.

And the chiefs forced their people that they should bring their magic things to her. And the Africans of some congregations supported her and slandered the UCCAR [United Church of Central Africa in Rhodesia]. At present she is the biggest leader in the Northern and North-Eastern Provinces in respect of witchcraft and prayers.

The number of pilgrims to Lenshina increased rapidly; in the dry season of 1956, up to 1,000 a week were counted. Her fame spread from her own tribe not only to their Rhodesian neighbours and into the Copperbelt, but also into Tanganyika, where Lenshina is said to have lived with her husband some time before her vision; and people in Nyasaland who heard about her crossed through some of the wildest country in the East of Northern Rhodesia in order to be baptized by her. Those who returned built small wattle-and-daub churches in which they held services "with a good deal of enthusiasm," in many places three times a week, singing the simple evangelical phrases which Lenshina had taught them, set to indigenous tunes, and listening to the self-appointed priests, many of whom were ex-mission catechists and teachers who had asked Lenshina's permission to pass on her message. . . .

The schism from the mission church was finalized by the end of 1958. The government had to recognize the new "church" as a *fait accompli.* It was presented with a declaration which showed clearly that the puritan reforming tendencies behind the message of Lenshina's vision were no deviation from the moral teachings, but rather a reinforcement of the strict rules, of the Church of Scotland Mission. The name "Lumpa Church" now occurs for the first time, and the explanation of the name varies. The church which "goes far," "excels all others," "hastens to Salvation." . . . The Laws of the Lumpa Church were formulated with the view of gaining the—hitherto withheld—approval of the Government after the strained relations of the trial period. They are still the basis of instruction. The Nchanga leader showed us a copy which was identical with that in the file of the District Commissioner at Chinsali:

1. Lumpa Church is an organisation in which to worship God and his son Jesus Christ. It is not an organisation to make unruly behaviour with the laws of the country.
2. In this organisation there shall be no racial discrimination, white and black men and women shall be Brotherhood and love each other.
3. Every Christian must not be in the following habits: (a) Back biting (b) insult (c) lies (d) pride (e) boasting (f) hatred (g) anger (h) harsh (i) false witness (j) selfish (k) rudeness (l) cunning (m) stealing and etc. He must be sincere, kind, trustworthy, love, patient and truthful.
4. Every Christian must keep away from the following: coveting, witchcraft, stealing, adultery, sorcery, witches, drunkenness, bad songs and all primitive dances. . . .

We were very glad to hear that during our study of Nchanga, Lenshina had come on one of her frequent visits to the Copperbelt and was actually staying in the camp of the railway workers in Chingola. We asked for an interview and received an invitation.

In the following five days we saw that Lenshina herself was keen to stress the rule of her church: No racial discrimination. Some of her staff, especially three or four of the leading men in Copperbelt congregations of the Lumpa Church, showed signs of uneasiness about our intrusion into the inner circle which surrounded the prophetess constantly during her public appearances and also most of the time when she rested. But no one made an attempt to hinder us in any way. Lenshina was the undisputed head of the group. "We have to ask Mama" repeatedly proved the answer to a request. Her quiet but unmistakably firm authority reminded me of a young woman who is the head of a Lunda village in the Luapula province. Even if the rumours are true that Lenshina had fits and other signs of spirit possession during her adolescence—and the African Roman Catholic priests of Illondola said that they received this information from Lenshina's own mother—the prophetess, now in her early thirties, looks a healthy, rather plump and happily relaxed village matron, a chief in her own right, as other women in her cultural stratum of matrilineal Bantu are chiefs through heritage. She is certainly not a medium, or psychopath, used by ruthless and politically ambitious men, as some have described her. Her sense of vocation is the firm foundation upon which her work is built. . . .

The most important medium in the Lumpa congregations is not the spoken but the sung word. In the Copperbelt, the singing processions in the African Townships have become a feature as well-known as the Salvation Army bands in Britain, and everybody recognises the peculiar Lenshina tunes. When asked about the origin of the hymns, the local Lumpa Church secretary said: "The One who let us have this church is the One who gives us the hymns; they come through Lenshina and she teaches them all over the country." With a group of young choir girls and her own two women attendants, Lenshina led the singing in the processions and during the services which we attended. When we made tape-recordings, we found that even the most informal sounding texts were really set—Lenshina clapped her hand over mouth and laughed when she made a mistake in a repetition—and one of the choir girls explained to us that all the tunes except one were old well-known Bemba ones, the odd one having been sung by the Chokwe when they visited Lenshina at Kasomo's village. . . .

The shortest of such hymns was sung when the procession in the Buchi African township passed the newly built beerhall. It is probably one of the oldest of Lenshina's choruses, with its simple statement of the two main "taboos," or reform rules of her movement:

Shout to the desert, shout:
Leave beer and witchcraft.

The call to repent is the main theme, but the sins of the lost sheep which the hymns mention are not simply the use of witchcraft and charms, or disregard for church rules on beer drinking or polygyny; although social misbehaviour is certainly termed sin, the fundamental sin, separation from God and contempt of the Saviour, is more frequently mentioned.

God says: Come to me, my children,
Go, and find the sheep,
the lost sheep,
I will restore them. . . .

Lenshina had told us at the beginning of the first interview that only she baptized. . . . At the beginning of each service, those who wished to be baptized were called to sit in front, and to take their hats and headscarves off—another reminiscence of Free Church practice. After introductory hymns and prayers, Ba Smart, the teacher, knelt in front of Lenshina and offered her a tin, covered with a simply embroidered white cloth. She also knelt and took it and removed the lid, which still bore the name of a well-known brand of floor polish. The water was in a glass jar in the tin. She took the jar carefully out of the carrier, wrapped it with the cloth, and proceeded to the kneeling congregation. Ba Smart asked the name of the person, then Lenshina dipped her fingers into the water and laid her hand on the head. She did not seem to say anything at all. Ba Smart also laid his hand on. . . .

The most impressive part of Lenshina's work followed the Sunday service. After a very short interval, in which she supervised the preparation of a meal for her European visitor and also had some food herself with her children and her woman companions, she spent over five hours in receiving visitors in the small living-room of a standard two-roomed African hut. The room was crammed with people of her entourage, the nannie for her children, her chauffeur, the girl singers and several deacons. One of the black-gowned "ministers" entered the names of the applicants in a book. I did not see anybody giving money or other presents. Small groups of twos and threes entered, knelt down to greet the prophetess and us with the polite formal clapping of their hands, others less formally shaking hands. The first was a blind man, with bad scars from smallpox, telling Lenshina how he had caught the disease in the Congo. A young man showed to her injuries on his leg caused by a fall off a bicycle. A mother handed her a baby and explained that the child had dysentery. Lenshina listened attentively, asked a few questions about the circumstances, and dismissed the patient without any promise of help or prayer, nor did she make any special gesture such as the laying-on of hands or touching the wounds. But one could clearly see the relief which the people felt when telling her about their troubles, and their gladness to be admitted to her presence. . . .

Is Lenshina regarded as a semi-divine being? There is nothing in the so-called constitution or in any of her proclamations which indicates such a claim. Her status is in many respects similar to that of a woman chief. In her village, her simple house with its outbuildings of kitchen, grainstore and dovecot is surrounded by a stockade like a chief's; she receives the respectful greeting with kneeling and clapping, and though a young woman is called Mama, i.e., grandmother. Like any chief, she is given presents of food and money, and these must have been very considerable to make the purchase of building materials and lorries possible. Newspaper reports said that on her last Copperbelt visit, the congregation gave her a gold wrist watch. The labour which was organized to build the "cathedral" followed the pattern of customary service for a chief; whole villages went to Kasomo's for four days at a time, bringing their own food and supplementary supplies for the sick and other pilgrims. It is not extraordinary to find a woman in such high position in the customary social organization of the Bemba, with their "mothers of the chiefs," the princesses who are sometimes ruling chiefs in their own right, the women guardians of the babenye, the holy tribal relics. But these offices are inherited, whereas Lenshina's status has been acquired by vocation, the divine vision and the special power of healing inherent in her since she "came back from the dead." In the eyes of her people she is therefore more than a woman of customary high status. "We know no Government, we know no chief, we only know Lenshina," shouted some Nyasaland villagers when they were told to pull down Lumpa church buildings they had erected. A District Officer wrote in 1955: "The extent of her following—60,000 pilgrims to her village in one year—is an indication of how unsatisfying the modern missionary approach to witchcraft is for the majority of Africans. Lenshina does not say that witchcraft is nonsense, but that she has been given the power to neutralize it."

26 / THE CHRISTIAN FAMILY IN NON-WESTERN CULTURE

In the struggle of Christianity to make itself more fully Asian or African the most persistent and central issues are those which have to do with family life, the relations of husband and wife and the training and initiation of children. In the nineteenth century most non-Western Christianity was ready to accept the Western standards in these matters as the Christian ones. Little thought was given as to what should be the truly Christian standards of judgment. By the middle of the twentieth century Christians of Asia and Africa were convinced that Western norms could not be adopted wholesale in this or any other area of non-Western culture. A fresh attempt was made to determine the ways in which Christians should guide their decisions on such matters.

African marriage, particularly in regard to polygamy, is the most notable example of such long-term imposition and fresh questioning. For the first time, African Christians are asking whether they should maintain the Western family patterns or should develop new ones more akin to their own traditions. The fact that they do not all arrive at the same answers indicates that the essence of indigenization—thinking for themselves—has taken place. Two selections are given below which show some of the variety of thought. The first is from the conclusions reached at a meeting held in 1963 by the All Africa Conference of Churches, an organization representing the major Protestant bodies of the continent. The proposal by this group for the acceptance of the bride price (a doubtful term) and of polygamists into the Church marks a revolutionary change from the usual past practice. The second is from the discussions and resolutions of three hundred African women who gathered in Togo in 1958 for a seminar of the World Union of Catholic Women's Organizations. It shows what educated women are thinking about marriage.

TWO CHRISTIAN STATEMENTS ON AFRICAN MARRIAGE

Statement on Bride Price and Polygamy

Justification for the continuance of the custom of bride price [the gifts given by the groom or his family to the bride's family] depends upon the form it takes in this modern and changing society. . . . In some cases, cupidity and greed have crept in, especially with the development of a cash economy. The token has changed into a financial transaction which not only places an unjustifiable burden on the family of the man, often sending him into marriage loaded with debt, but also turns the woman into a chattel, thus diminishing her integrity as an individual. Such a version of bride price can lead to resentment by the man, to a commercial assessment of the conduct, work and value of the woman, to harsh decisions on the position of a wife, particularly in relation to her children, if the marriage should break up. . . .

The Church, however, is unlikely to achieve anything good simply by legislating that bride price should be abolished. If the Church preaches the word of God, with its message of the dignity of man and woman and marriage, and if Christians take this word to heart and practice it, bride price will disappear slowly from among them by itself, and die a natural death; as indeed it appears already to be doing in some areas and under some conditions. Many would wish to hurry the process. It will naturally linger in the more stable, rural communities. It will be less likely to survive in the changing pattern of urban life, and in the more sophisticated areas where bonds of extended families tend to weaken and where the characteristic family unit is one of father, mother, and their own children. The influence of the State is more likely to be effective when

From *Report of the All Africa Seminar on the Christian Home and Family Life* (Kitwe, Zambia: All Africa Council of Churches, 1963), pp. 16-17, 21-22. Reprinted by permission of the publisher.

it aims at limiting the abuses of bride price, rather than at attacking the institution itself.

Now as one of the advantages of the bride price was that, when it had been paid, the marriage was regarded as having been agreed upon and concluded by both partners and their families, it is strongly felt that it should if possible be retained in the form of some symbol, which would seal the contract and would witness to the solemnity of the union being entered into. This symbol could be in the form of an exchange between the two partners or their families, as a present or covenant token; and it would be followed by the Christian rites at the marriage itself. . . .

Steps which the Church could take towards the
elimination of polygamy:

These measures must be gradual, and they must have regard to the causes of polygamy.

1. Good sex education and marriage counselling for teachers, church-workers, youth, engaged couples, people in the early years of marriage, and for older couples.

2. Organization (in co-operation with the State) of courses of education, in community centres, in matters of sex.

3. To encourage the early seeking of competent medical advice in apparently childless marriages and to promote the establishment of clinics for the treatment of venereal diseases, in order to reduce the incidence of sterility.

4. To work for an improved rural economy, and the fostering of better agriculture by means of co-operatives, the use of agricultural machinery etc., instead of a plurality of wives.

5. To teach good methods of family planning, and of the feeding of infants. . . .

Recommendations:

1. That a pagan polygamist on conversion be received into the Church, his wives and his children.
2. That the position of monogamous Christians who become polygamists be carefully studied; and that each case be judged on its merits.
3. That exclusion from the Holy Communion be no longer employed as a means of discipline.
4. That persons excluded by the Church have still a claim on its pastoral responsibility.

5. That the Church should scrutinize any Government legislation designed to discourage or eliminate polygamy, with regard to both its short-term and its long-term effects.

African Women Speak

Everyone could tell a story of the difficulties, some serious, some merely annoying, which arise from the extended family system, but no one suggested abandoning it.

While it is irritating to have one's sisters-in-law walk unbidden into the house at any time, feeling free to help themselves from "my brother's fridge," there is also a sense of well-being and pleasure in having many "brothers and sisters"—i.e., cousins, uncles, aunts.

One of the more serious handicaps, some delegates pointed out, is the financial burden a man has in regard to his sister's children. Often because of this he may find it impossible to educate his own children.

On the other hand, the extended family is an African institution which lends itself to Christianity, since it offers the opportunity to practice the virtue of charity.

The small family unit of mother, father and children has advantages in the development of close family relationship insofar as it emphasizes the father's duty to his wife and children and makes more necessary and possible the practice of the Christian concept of mutual rights and responsibilities.

The happy solution for African families would be a blend of the two systems—emphasizing the primary responsibilities of husband, wife and children to one another, but extending their responsibilities to other members of the family. . . .

There was unanimous emphasis that the young girl of marriageable age must have the right to choose her husband, although she should not ignore the wise advice that her parents give her. She should be careful to choose a young man whose education and interests are similar to her own. This will be a help in trying to achieve a stable marriage.

It is a girl's duty to resist the pressures of her family when they try to make her marry a man who already has one or more wives.

Many unhappy cases were cited of difficulties in marriages between an educated man and an illiterate woman. A few of these remain happily married. But if the husband enters public life or a professional field, he

From *African Women Speak*. Regional Seminar of World Union of Catholic Women's Organizations. Edited by the National Catholic Welfare Conference Office for United Nations Affairs (Maryknoll, New York: Maryknoll Publications, 1960), pp. 69-70, 113-14. Reprinted by permission of the publisher.

is often tempted to send away his illiterate wife in order to marry one who can serve as his hostess. If he does not actually divorce the first, he still may take a second wife (and this raises the problem of polygamy again), or he may make one or two concubines his hostesses and companions to public functions. While this problem will disappear with the expansion of education for women, it is painful and humiliating for any discarded wife, and a serious problem for the Catholic wife. . . .

Considering with regret that in Africa marriage is a contract concluded between two family groups rather than between two people, and considering that this conception of marriage envisages primarily the benefit of the families, and does not take into sufficient consideration the wishes of the interested parties who are obliged in some cases to accept against their will a partner they have not chosen themselves, and whom they would refuse if they were free to do so, and considering that the bride price as it exists at present in certain African territories is a major obstacle to the freedom of the young girl and deprives many young men of the fundamental right to contract a legitimate marriage, the seminar participants ask

> for the complete suppression of the custom of promising in marriage girls who have not yet attained the age of puberty,
>
> that the custom of beginning to pay the bride price (whether this consists of money, gifts, or labor) for a girl who has not attained the age of puberty, should be absolutely forbidden,
>
> that the bride price should never be allowed to be an obstacle to a normal marriage, and that it should take on a symbolism in those regions where it is considered necessary to maintain the custom; that all the abuses brought about by the bride price custom, which lower marriage to the level of a purely business arrangement, should be legally suppressed; and that mention of the bride price should not be obligatory in the civil contract,
>
> for the suppression of polygamy, which gravely prejudices the dignity and the rights of woman and prevents the normal education and development of the child,
>
> that it should be made legally possible for a monogamous married couple to have property common to both husband and wife and which the children may inherit later on,
>
> that in case of the death of the husband, the widow should be the guardian of those of her children who are still minors,

that indissoluble and monogamous marriage freely contracted should be recognized as the only kind from which will rise the strong and healthy generations which Africa needs to fulfill her destiny. . . .

27 / RESPONSIBILITY IN SOCIETY

As Christianity has become more thoroughly rooted in the non-Western world and expresses itself more consciously as an element of non-Western life, it has evidenced, understandably enough, a growing social concern. The non-Western world is faced with such gigantic social problems at the present time that those who would participate fully in its life are forced to adopt a high level of social responsibility. Christians want it to be clearly understood that they are full members of the developing countries in which they live, that they rejoice in their citizenship in those lands and desire to play their full part as citizens. When they have been attacked as a divisive minority with Western connections they have reacted vigorously. Numerous conferences and declarations have expressed their involvement in the efforts to unify, modernize, and strengthen their societies.

The Christians of India exemplify this direction of thought and action. They are among the most zealous in desiring to take their part in society. They have also had to meet the typical opposition from critics who accuse them of having no place in the life of the country. Their notable leadership in political affairs is doubtless the most convincing answer to such opponents. All of these activities and attitudes are clearly reflected in the following report from an outstanding Indian Christian who has been deeply involved in recent events as Archbishop of Bangalore and General Secretary of the Catholic Bishop's Conference of India.

Christianity in a Free India

On August 15, 1947, India attained freedom and independence. With the people of our immense country, Catholics rejoiced in the hard-won triumph that culminated more than a half-century struggle. The battle had not been one of arms, but of ideologies; and on that battleground India's national aspirations had surpassed British genius and ingenuity. . . .

From Thomas Pothacamury, *The Church in Independent India* (Maryknoll, New York: Maryknoll Publications, n.d.), pp. 4-5, 14, 18, 26, 28-29. Reprinted by permission of the publisher.

Anticipating the achievement of national independence, the Catholic Bishops' Conference of July, 1947 acclaimed the spirit of good will and cordiality between the British Government and the Indian statesmen in reaching the momentous agreement. . . .

The statement of the hierarchy included an exhortation to all Catholics "to give their best to the motherland, to serve as a bond of union among sections which may be kept apart from one another by suspicion or discord, and to avail themselves of every opportunity to foster a sense of unity and solidarity, so that peace, brotherly love and happiness may reign among all. . . ." And their words were echoed by all of India's Catholics—priests, Brothers, Sisters and members of the laity—who felt an immense joy and pride in the emancipation of their country from colonial rule. . . .

Immediately after India attained independence in 1947, there was a noticeable feeling of friendliness among almost all classes of Indians toward Christianity and its missionaries. The foreign missionaries did not leave the country with the British, but remained at their posts and carried on their work with the same zeal as before. They showed in every way complete loyalty towards the Indian Government.

More recently, however, a change has come about. The anti-Christian slogans of bigoted and chauvinistic groups have been echoed by a section of the Indian press, and have influenced the minds of certain segments of the population. As a result, a degree of antagonism towards Christians has developed. . . .

One of the most disturbing weapons directed against the Church by extreme Hindu nationalists has been the organization of official inquiry committees. In 1954, the State Government of Madhya Pradesh, in central India, appointed a six-man committee to investigate Christian missionary activities in that State.

The activities of the committee soon gave rise to wide-spread comment in the Indian press. For this reason, the Standing Committee of the Catholic Bishops' Conference of India, which was in session at Bangalore, addressed a memorandum on June 15, 1954 to the Chief Minister of the Government of Madhya Pradesh. In moderate but firm language, the Catholic Bishops pointed out that five members of the investigating committee were Hindus. The only Christian member, a man who did not believe in the divinity of Christ, had no representative status in the Christian community. Inasmuch as the emphasis of the Madhya Pradesh Inquiry Committee's work was on alleged abuses committed by the missionaries, the Bishops expressed their doubts as to the committee's impartiality.

Undeterred by the Bishops' protest, the Madhya Pradesh Inquiry Committee continued its work in partisan fashion. Its report, which was not published until 1956, created a sensation throughout India. For the committee condemned roundly the efforts of Catholic and Protestant missionaries among the poor and illiterate aboriginal tribesmen of the state's remote rural areas. It accused the missionaries of making conversions to Christianity through cost-free lessons, the gift of school books, ploughs, oxen and the loan of money. The converts, it was alleged in the report, became "denaturalized" and strangers to their own country, for the main aim of the missionaries was to create a "Christian Party" or "State within a State." And fear was expressed that one day the Christian community would assert its right to form a separate state as had the Moslems of Pakistan. The report recommended that the Central Government should consider the following steps: ordering the missionaries to leave the country; severely controlling conversions and baptisms; prohibiting by law the use of medical assistance as an instrument of the apostolate; and amending the Constitution so as to limit the right of propagating religion to Indian nationals.

The Madhya Pradesh Inquiry Committee report has done much to embitter relations between India's non-Christian majority and its Christian minority. . . .

In October, 1955, local leaders of the Hindu Mahasabha movement attacked the Catholic church at Vardhaman Nagar, a village in the state of Bihar. Interrupting the sacrifice of the Mass, the insurgents beat up the priest and members of the congregation, threw them bodily out of the church, and proceeded to desecrate the building. The police arrested the responsible parties, who were condemned by a court to prison terms.

Mr. Nehru, India's Prime Minister, later informed Parliament how shocked he had been by this brutal attack on a harmless priest and his flock. He referred to the incident as "a most disgraceful occurrence. . . ."

On other occasions, Mr. Nehru has not hesitated to speak out against the anti-Christian position of extreme Hindu nationalist groups. On August 9, 1954, for example, he criticized the Hindu Mahasabha to Congress Party leaders of the various states in these words:

"The tendency in some parts of India to adopt an aggressive attitude towards Christian missionaries is to be deplored. . . . It encourages a narrow and bigoted approach to a problem which should be dealt with calmly at the national level." He urged Congress Party members to bear in mind that "minority religious communities in India, such as Moslems, Christians, Sikhs, Parsis, Buddhists, Jains, Jews, etc., are as much a part of India as anyone else. . . ."

Christians, sharing in the political life of the nation, have frequently supported the Congress Party at the polls. A number of Catholics have run for office on the Congress Party ticket; others have been associated with the Praja-Socialist Party, a democratic party whose position is similar to that of the British Labour Party.

In the 1957 general elections, twenty-one Christians were returned to the Kerala State Assembly. Fourteen of them were Catholics who stood on the Congress Party list; another Catholic was supported by the Praja-Socialist Party; and the remaining six Christians were non-Catholics.

In the same election, four Catholics and five Protestants won with the Congress Party ticket in Madras State. One of the Catholics, Mrs. Lourdamma Simon, was appointed State Minister for Local Administration and Fisheries. She is a former teacher in a Catholic school, and was for three years head of the Legion of Mary in Kottar Diocese.

The people of Andra State selected two Catholics for its Assembly in the 1957 elections. In Mysore State a Catholic was returned on the Congress Party ticket, while another Catholic won out as an Independent. The Deputy Minister for Education in Mysore is a Protestant Christian.

Meanwhile, the Congress Party, true to the tolerant principles of its top leaders, has entrusted responsible positions to Christians. Two Protestants are members of the Central Government's cabinet: Miss Rajkumari Amrit Kaur, Minister of Health; and Mr. John Matthai, Minister of Finance. The former Governor of Bombay, Raja Sir Maharaja Singh, is a Protestant; and the late Mr. H. C. Mukerjee, Governor of West Bengal, was also a Protestant. Recently, Mr. A. J. John, a devout Catholic and former Chief Minister of Kerala State, was appointed Governor of Madras.

Such appointments as these do not usually receive headlines in the secular press of India and other countries. Unlike the sensational news of the Madhya Pradesh Inquiry Committee, they pass almost unnoticed. Yet, in their own way, they signify both India's political maturity and the extent to which India's Christians are trusted and respected by their fellowmen. . . .

28 / PIONEERS OF CHRISTIAN UNITY

Non-Western Christianity has not been content simply to try to break loose from the domination and leadership of the Western Churches. It has essayed to take the lead itself and to break the path along which Western Christendom should follow. Some of the expressions of social responsibility coming from Asian and African Christians have asserted the inadequacy of Western thought and action in this realm and proposed more adequate positions. More generally recognized as a challenge to the West has been the leadership of Asian and African churches in the cause of Christian unity. It was in India and China, in the nineteenth century, that some of the earliest and most important forerunners of the modern ecumenical movement appeared. The International Missionary Conference in Edinburgh in 1910 was the crystallization of that movement. The demands of Asia and Africa loomed large among the reasons for calling the recent Ecumenical Council of the Roman Catholic Church.

The most far-reaching accomplishments in Christian unity are the united churches which have appeared primarily in the non-Western world. Starting at the beginning of the twentieth century, these have increased both in number and in the breadth of ecclesiastical bodies which they have encompassed. The best known is the Church of South India, which was the first to bind together the radically Protestant, congregationally organized churches with the more catholic, hierarchically organized churches. The following selection comes from the pen of one of the leading laymen of that Church and suggests both the joy and enthusiasm which it has engendered and the clear conviction that the West must follow its example.

The Church of South India

It was in the providence of God that, soon after the declaration of political independence, something should happen which opened a new era in the history of Christianity in this country. This was the inauguration of the Church of South India on the 27th of September 1947 in St. George's Cathedral, Madras, hailed variously as a "venture of faith," "a momentous achievement in unity," "the greatest step forward in Church unity in modern times," "a beacon in our Christian World" and also as "a schism deliberately planned and carried through."

From Rajaiah D. Paul, *The First Decade: An Account of the Church of South India* (Madras: The Christian Literature Society, 1958), pp. 14, 1-4. Reprinted by permission of the author and of the publisher.

To us here in India it was a day of great rejoicing but also a day of great expectations. Not only had it pleased God to bless the endeavours of His people and to give them that much-longed-for unity which would begin the process of healing the wounds on the Body of Christ; but He had also placed on this new Church an onerous task of leading the rest of Christendom in a great spiritual adventure for God. . . .

It was not with any utilitarian motives or for any pragmatic reasons that the Churches in South India entered into this union. It is true that it was being increasingly felt that the divisions in the Church were impeding the spread of Christianity in the land; and that not only in India but everywhere in the world the witness of the Church was to a large extent being nullified by its dividedness. The Christian Gospel is "an invitation to all men all over the world to meet as one family," at the foot of the Cross of Jesus Christ, where and where only they can meet as members of one family because they have all obtained the forgiveness of the one-Father and have been accepted by Him as His children. Those who give this invitation and seek to spread that Gospel must needs show in their own lives—as groups and as Churches—that they are living as one family. If the Christian Gospel is true, there can be nothing that tends to divide them—belief, practice, ritual—which cannot be overcome by their overwhelming and adoring love of God in Christ. If the invitation that they give is to be compelling they cannot give it in a state of division. "The disunity of Christians is a public contradiction of the Gospel. . . ."

But even so, the compulsion towards union came not from strategy but from an inner conviction that unity is the will of God for the Church and that disunity is sin. It was clear to the leaders of the Churches in South India that the Holy Spirit was definitely leading them towards unity and that that guidance was not to be thwarted except at great spiritual peril. "We believe that union is the will of God," was the declaration made in the famous Tranquebar manifesto. The Rt. Rev. Michael Hollis wrote in *The Spectator* of September 26, 1947 (the day before the Inauguration of the C.S.I.), "Fundamentally, we seek to be one because Christ prayed 'that they may all be one . . . that the world may believe that thou didst send me.' "

The union was entered into in obedience to this irresistible conviction that unity is the will of God for the Church and that whatever might have been the reasons which justified, at the time and for the time being, the divisions which arose in the Church, to stay apart would be sinful disobedience to God's will.

> In obedience to the Lord Jesus Christ, the Head of the Church, and by the authority of the governing bodies of the uniting churches, I do hereby declare that these three churches are become one Church of South India.

was the announcement which the Presiding Bishop made at the Inauguration service. . . .

The Inauguration of the Church of South India was also intended to be something far more momentous than the achievement of a merely local union. The new Church expected great things to happen, both in South India and throughout the Christian world, because it had come into existence. The union was intended to be the first step towards the reunion of all the Churches throughout the world, and to lead ultimately to the spiritual unification of the whole of Christendom. This was what was put into the Constitution.

> The Church of South India acknowledges that in every effort to bring together divided members of Christ's body into one organization, the final aim must be the union in the Universal Church of all who acknowledge the name of Christ.

It is just because the union was designed to have a far wider effect than the formation of a new Church in South India that it attracted so much attention and produced so much jubilation on one side and so much heart-searching on the other. A new Church of the type and nature of the Church of South India having come into existence, the other Churches of Christendom could no longer be just interested lookers-on; they were necessarily challenged to some action on their own part. As the Moderator pointed out in his address to the Second (1950) Synod:

> The very fact that we exist provides an inescapable challenge to the other Churches. The obvious irritation with which the C.S.I. is regarded in certain quarters is a proof of the disquiet which we have caused, by our uniting, among those who prefer church union to remain as an item on the agenda of a long series of conferences. The whole question of union can never be the same again after what happened in Madras on September 27, 1947. More and more it must become clear that it is not we in our union who are the anomaly, but the disunited churches here and abroad which still too largely look upon a divided church as the normal condition of those who profess their faith in the same God, the same Saviour, the same Holy Spirit.

Secondly, the Church hoped to make itself "a more effective instrument for God's work" than were any of its constituent Churches in their separation. It hoped that very early in its life, there would come greater peace, closer fellowship and a fuller life within the Church and that there would come renewed eagerness and power for the proclamation of the Gospel of Christ. It hoped that it might be "a true leaven of unity in the life of India and that through it there might be a greater release of divine power throughout the world for the fulfilment of God's purpose for His world."

But it did not conceive of itself as a consummation, a completed achievement. Nor does it even now think of itself as something permanent and immutable. From the very beginning the Church of South India made it clear that when the next step came to be taken—the creation of a single united Church for South India—it would be prepared to die in order to become a live part of a real Church of South India. It was determined from the first to engage itself in an unflagging attempt to widen and strengthen the fellowship between itself and its parent Churches and "to work towards the goal of the full union in one body of all parts of the Church of Christ." From the very beginning the Church of South India also considered itself to be a Church on the move and has refused to be bound down by any tradition or usage or to settle down to any fixed pattern. "The idea of movement is written into its fundamental documents," and it is in a very real sense a Pilgrim Church, a Church on the wing, a Church ready to immolate itself on the altar of a wider unity.

CONCLUSION

The long conversation between the Christian faith and the non-Western world is not completed, but its terms are rapidly changing. As has been evident, the topics for discussion have until recently clustered around the implications of Western-based Christian faith for Eastern patterns of life and, conversely, the impact of Eastern patterns on this Western-based Christianity. This dialogue has largely determined the nature of non-Western Christianity. As the variety of readings has shown, the resultant religion has been of an exceedingly diverse and varied kind, suggesting the changing weight of the parties in the discussion from place to place and century to century.

But recently there has been a significant change in the conversation. Christianity has been breaking with the idea that it depends on a Western base and has been asserting its Eastern identity. At the same time the Eastern world with which it seeks to come to terms has become highly Westernized. From now on the topics for discussion will be centered as

much on the implications of Eastern-based Christianity for Western pat-
terns of life as on the older questions. The fact that the two major con-
frontations of the recent period have been those with nationalism and
Communism, both products of the West, is an indication of the change.

Its new freedom and indigenous nature, however, should enable non-
Western Christianity to speak to both the Western and Eastern elements
of its environment on its own initiative and terms and not as an echo of
Western Christendom. They should also enable it to speak to the West
from an equal footing and to cooperate with the West on an equal basis.
This, in fact, is what is happening as increasing numbers of non-Western
churches join the World Council of Churches and as Asian and African
voices are increasingly heard in Roman Catholic councils. Not only is
this taking place in connection with the churches of Western provenance;
the ancient Asian and African churches which represent the East in its
most independent and most isolated form are also coming out from be-
hind their walls and entering into closer contact with the West.

The point to which our story has led us, then, seems to be the point
at which non-Western Christianity has come of age, but also the point
at which it is beginning to lose its more distinctive existence through in-
volvement in a larger field of relationships. From this point on it be-
comes more difficult to identify a non-Western Christianity, just as it be-
comes more difficult to identify a non-Western world. The direction is
toward one Christianity, as it is toward one world.

FURTHER READINGS

In addition to the books which are noted as sources for the readings, the following works are recommended for further information and bibliographical guidance in the field of non-Western Church history.

General Histories

Latourette, Kenneth Scott, *A History of the Expansion of Christianity*. 7 volumes. New York: Harper and Brothers, 1937-45. The standard work in the field, with full bibliographies for each country and period.

Neill, Stephen, *A History of Christian Missions*. Baltimore, Maryland: Penguin Books, Inc., 1964. A one-volume history available in paperback. Thoroughly readable and reliable. Contains up-to-date bibliographies.

de Vaulx, Bernard, *History of the Missions*. New York: Hawthorn Books, Inc., 1961. A history of Roman Catholic missions. Part of the "Twentieth Century Encyclopedia of Catholicism."

Bolshakoff, Serge, *The Foreign Missions of the Russian Orthodox Church*. London: Society for Promoting Christian Knowledge, 1943. The only general study of this field, though important studies of limited parts of it have been published.

Warneck, Gustav, *Outline of the History of Protestant Missions From the Reformation to the Present Time*. Edinburgh: J. Gemmell, 1884. An old work, largely superseded by Latourette, but still the only scholarly history of Protestant missions as a whole.

The Medieval and Early Modern Periods

Arpee, Leon, *A History of Armenian Christianity from the Beginning to Our Own Time*. New York: The Armenian Missionary Association of America, 1946. A comprehensive work.

Brown, Leslie W., *The Indian Christians of St. Thomas*. Cambridge: Cambridge

University Press, 1956. A contemporary description with coverage of the earlier history.

Perham, Margary, *The Government of Ethiopia*. London: Faber & Faber, Ltd., 1948. Chapter VII gives an excellent introduction to the present Church and refers to the standard literature on its history.

Peers, E. A., *Ramon Lull, a Biography*. New York: The Macmillan Company, 1929. The principal biography of the best known of medieval missionaries to the non-Western world.

Foster, John, *The Church of the T'ang Dynasty*. London: Society for Promoting Christian Knowledge, 1939. Covers the eastern spread of Christianity till about 900 A.D.

Moule, A. C. *Christians in China Before the Year 1550*. New York: The Macmillan Company, 1930. Completes the medieval story.

Plattner, Felix, *Jesuits Go East*. Dublin: Clonmore and Reynolds, 1950. Based on primary sources but as readable as a novel. Covers the Jesuit exploits in Asia through the eighteenth century.

Brodrick, James, *St. Francis Xavier, 1506-1552*. New York: Wicklow Press, 1952. A large and well written biography.

Rowbotham, Arnold H., *Missionary and Mandarin. The Jesuits at the Court of China*. Berkeley and Los Angeles: University of California Press, 1942. Excellent historical treatment.

Area Histories (with emphasis on the nineteenth and twentieth centuries)

Africa

Groves, C. P., *The Planting of Christianity in Africa*. 4 volumes. London: Lutterworth Press, 1948-58. The only full history for the continent as a whole.

Du Plessis, J., *A History of Christian Missions in South Africa*. London: Longmans, Green & Company, Ltd., 1911. A basic work, supplemented in 1958 by G. B. A. Gerdener's *Recent Developments in the South African Mission Field*. London and Edinburgh: Marshall, Morgan & Scott.

Hinchcliff, Peter, *The Anglican Church in South Africa. An Account of the History and Development of the Church of the Province of South Africa*. London: Darton, Longman & Todd, 1963. Illuminates much of the activity of the Church as a whole in Africa.

Slade, Ruth N., *English-speaking Missions in the Congo Independent State (1878-1908)*. Brussels: 1959. A careful piece of historical reconstruction.

Kittler, Glenn D., *The White Fathers*. New York: Harper and Brothers, 1957. The story of the first and most prominent of Roman Catholic orders devoted to Africa. Reissued 1961 in paperback.

Oliver, Roland, *The Missionary Factor in East Africa*. London and New York: Longmans, Green & Company, Ltd., 1952. The relation of missions to political developments.

Sundkler, Bengt G. M., *Bantu Prophets in South Africa*. London: Oxford University Press, 1948, 2nd ed., 1961. The pioneer study of the independent churches which have grown up in Africa.

Desai, Ram, *Christianity in Africa as Seen by Africans*. Denver, Colorado: Alan Swallow, 1962. An example of the recent nationalist critique of Christianity.

China

Latourette, Kenneth Scott, *A History of Christian Missions in China*. London: Society for Promoting Christian Knowledge, 1929. A massive and scholarly work.

Boardman, Eugene, *Christian Influence Upon the Ideology of the Taiping Rebellion, 1851-1864*. Madison: University of Wisconsin Press, 1952. The most recent reexamination of the evidence on this rebellion.

Varg, Paul, *Missionaries, Chinese and Diplomats. The American Protestant Missionary Movement in China, 1890-1952*. Princeton, New Jersey: Princeton University Press, 1958. A highly useful though not always understanding treatment.

Jones, Francis P., *The Church in Communist China*. New York: Friendship Press, 1962. A brief but judicious handling of the recent history.

India

Richter, Julius, *A History of Missions in India*. New York: F. H. Revell Co., 1908. Designed as a full history, but weak on Roman Catholic developments.

Firth, Cyril, *An Introduction to Indian Church History*. Madras: Christian Literature Society, 1961. A more recent and topical coverage.

Ingham, Kenneth, *Reformers in India 1793-1833. An Account of the Work of Christian Missionaries on Behalf of Social Reform*. Cambridge: Cambridge University Press, 1956. Concise and impartial. On the reformist activities of the early nineteenth-century missionaries.

Sundkler, Bengt, *The Church of South India: The Movement Toward Union 1900-1947*. London: Lutterworth Press, 1954. The major history of this movement.

Japan

Cary, Otis, *A History of Christianity in Japan*. 2 volumes. New York: F. H. Revell Co., 1909. The only complete history of Roman Catholic, Russian Orthodox, and Protestant work. Now somewhat out of date.

Boxer, C. R., *The Christian Century in Japan 1549-1650*. Berkeley and Los Angeles: University of California Press, and London: Cambridge University

Press, 1951. Already listed as a source in the readings, but of such importance as to require its inclusion here.

Van Hecken, Joseph, *The Catholic Church in Japan Since 1859*. Tokyo: Herder Agency, 1963. An institutional history.

Iglehart, Charles, *A Century of Protestant Christianity in Japan*. Tokyo and Rutland, Vermont: Charles E. Tuttle, 1959. A well written centennial history.

Korea

Paik, Lark-June George, *The History of Protestant Missions in Korea, 1832-1910*. Pyeng Yong: Union Christian College Press, 1929. A detailed study of the final twenty-five years covered.

The Middle East

Attwater, Donald, *The Christian Churches of the East*. 2 volumes. Milwaukee: Bruce Publishing Co., 1935, 1947. On the history and present condition of the ancient churches. The first volume covers those in communion with Rome and the second those that are not.

Addison, J. T., *The Christian Approach to the Moslem, a Historical Study*. New York: Columbia University Press, 1942. A careful historical analysis, from medieval times to the present.

Joseph, John, *The Nestorians and Their Muslim Neighbors. A Study of Western Influence on Their Relations*. Princeton, New Jersey: Princeton University Press, 1961. Deals with the nineteenth and twentieth centuries, showing the problems introduced by Western influence.

Oceania

Wright, Louis B., and Mary Fry, *Puritans in the South Seas*. New York: Henry Holt and Co., 1936. Covers the island missions. Based on original sources. Always debunks its subject matter.

Wright, Harrison M., *New Zealand 1769-1840; Early Years of Western Contact*. Contains much illuminating material on Christianity among other forms of Western contact.

OTHER SPECTRUM BOOKS OF INTEREST

The Asian Civilization Series

The Modern Nations in Historical Perspective Series

ARGENTINA, Arthur P. Whitaker—S-601
AUSTRALIA, Russel Ward—S-610
THE BALKANS, Charles Jelavich
and Barbara Jelavich—S-611
CENTRAL AMERICA, Mario Rodríguez—S-609
CEYLON, Sinnappah Arasaratnam—S-603
CHINA, Kenneth Scott Latourette—S-607
CUBA, HAITI, & THE DOMINICAN REPUBLIC,
John E. Fagg—S-615
FRANCE, John C. Cairns—S-617
INDIA, Stanley Wolpert—S-613
INDONESIA, J. D. Legge—S-606
ITALY, Massimo Salvadori—S-612
MOROCCO, ALGERIA, TUNISIA, Richard M. Brace—S-604
NEW ZEALAND, William J. Cameron—S-608
NIGERIA AND GHANA, John E. Flint—S-618
THE PHILIPPINES, Onofre D. Corpuz—S-616
RUSSIA, Robert V. Daniels—S-602
SCANDINAVIA, John H. Wuorinen—S-614
VENEZUELA AND COLOMBIA, Harry Bernstein—S-605